PENSION
SCHEMES

International Labour Office - Geneva

First published 1997

ISBN 92-2-110737-X

Author unit: SEC/PDN
Editor: T. Whitaker
Designer: P. Bissaca, E. Fortarezza
Production: International Training Centre of the ILO, Turin, Italy

PREFACE

This manual is one of a series produced by the Social Security Department of the International Labour Office, Geneva. It was prepared in conjunction with the International Training Centre of the ILO, Turin and the International Social Security Association, Geneva.

Other publications in the series:

- Social Security Principles
- Administration of Social Security
- Social Security Financing
- Social Health Insurance
- A Trainers' Guide

The manuals have been produced primarily for use in countries where social security systems are not yet operational, are undergoing change or need to be improved. In particular, the manuals will be useful in developing countries, countries in transition, and countries undergoing structural change, as they begin the process of setting up new systems of social protection or of improving existing systems.

It should be noted, however, that the information contained in the manuals refers almost entirely to the formal sector and not to the wide range of systems which apply to groups outside the traditional social security system.

It will be apparent that, in a manual of this size, it is possible to provide only a broad overview of the topic. For the reader needing more extensive or detailed information about pension schemes, there may well be a need for additional reading. There is a wide range of publications which deal with the topic in greater depth and some of these are referred to in the additional reading list at the end of this manual.

Thanks are due to all those people - too numerous to mention individually - who have helped in the preparation of this manual. In particular, the assistance of the International Social Security Association (ISSA) is acknowledged.

Should any reader wish to provide comments or feedback on the contents of this or any other manual in the series, please write to:

> The International Labour Office,
> SEC/SOC, 9th Floor,
> 4 route des Morillons,
> CH-1211 GENEVE 22,
> Switzerland.
> Fax (22) 799.7962

TABLE OF CONTENTS

PENSION SCHEMES

MODULE 1:
PUBLIC AND PRIVATE
PENSION SCHEMES

International Labour Office - Geneva

MODULE CONTENTS

MODULE 1

PUBLIC AND PRIVATE PENSION SCHEMES

UNIT 1: Methods of protection in public schemes

A. Pension schemes

National schemes of old-age, invalidity and survivor benefits, intended to protect large segments of the elderly and disabled population or those deprived of resources due to the death of the family breadwinner, have continued to develop and progress throughout the twentieth century. Emerging, although at different times, from common sources and origins — occupational retirement funds, assistance schemes and non-contributory pension schemes, voluntary insurance, corporate solidarity, mutual assistance funds and so on — these national schemes, which have now been made compulsory, have become solidly anchored in the social legislation of various countries. This has been done independently of the predominant political ideology or the economic, demographic and social context, and even of the level of development, since they are established in a very large majority of the world's countries.

At the present time, these schemes form the cornerstone of social protection systems everywhere.

The responses given to the need to ensure social protection for the population are extremely varied, not only from country to country but often even within a given country. The current systems are the outcome of multiple factors and bear the mark of the differences in economic, social, political and ideological backgrounds, historical conditions and the concerns and imagination of governments and their leaders.

Old-age, invalidity and survivors' benefits are usually in the form of pensions, i.e., long-term periodic payments. However, in some schemes the benefit may be a single payment. Pension schemes have often been the subject of debate, for example, over the level of benefits or the age of retirement. Currently, however, they are increasingly questioned regarding their effectiveness and future viability. The economic environment, demographic change, the emergence of new life styles and individual aspirations, are among the new realities that have focused attention on existing systems.

Although these schemes have been organized primarily by the State, public intervention in the field of pension protection has nevertheless been preceded by various initiatives: voluntary personal insurance and individual or perhaps group initiatives on the part of employers wanting to ensure labour stability and to bind workers to the enterprise by offering them a range of benefits, in particular old-age pensions. For this purpose, employers developed their own retirement funds.

The State was initially involved in organizing pensions in its position as an employer (pensions granted to civil servants) usually before bringing in legislation for other categories of workers. This occurred first in Germany, with the creation by Bismarck in 1889 of an invalidity and old-age insurance scheme for workers; this was followed by Denmark where the first non-contributory old-age benefits scheme was introduced in 1891.

Only rarely have the current schemes been set up all at once. They have been built up by successive additions and they are still evolving, which makes them extremely complex. In a single country one often finds, side by side, schemes based on different principles or applying to different categories of the population. Moreover, although the State continues to be the main agent everywhere, private initiative plays a significant role in numerous countries. On the other hand, although the extension of protection to all residents has now virtually been achieved in many countries, there are others where the scope of protection is still very limited.

A classification of pension schemes begins with the distinction between public and private schemes, between the various basic mechanisms or techniques that are applied, and between the general schemes and those which apply only to certain categories of workers. To adequately represent the situation in practice, it should be noted that various combinations of these elements have been developed.

B. *The various methods of protection in public schemes*

There are, with numerous variants, two major types of public pension schemes, which match the two basic concepts that have developed in the field of social protection. On the one hand, there are the social insurance schemes and, on the other, the non-contributory benefit schemes (financed by public funds) which are either universal or, where the idea of assistance continues to predominate, means-tested. To these two major types should be added a third, national provident funds, which are basically compulsory savings institutions and are found in a number of developing countries.

Fig. 1:
"... on the one hand, social insurance schemes: on the other, non-contributory schemes ... and provident funds ..."

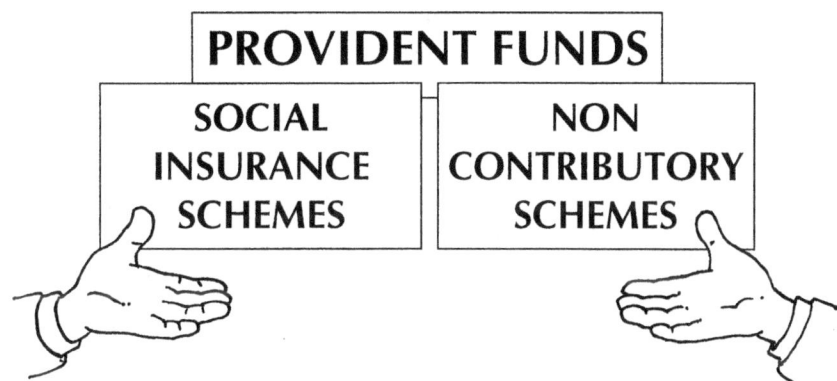

Social insurance schemes

At present, most schemes in the world are based on the principle of social insurance. After the first scheme of this type, set up in Germany in 1889, this model spread throughout most European countries. Between the two World Wars, it reached Latin America and North America and, after the Second World War, numerous countries in Africa, Asia and the Caribbean.

Social insurance is financed by contributions from the employer and in many cases also by the worker, with or without a subsidy from the State. Membership is compulsory for the occupational categories involved and, in certain countries, for the population as a whole. Pension entitlement and benefit amount are determined by the beneficiary's professional career (periods of contribution or employment) and by the beneficiary's earnings throughout his or her working life. The pension is paid without reference to need or income. In the majority of countries, contributions are received by independent funds which then pay out the benefits.

Non-contributory benefit schemes

In the non-contributory benefit schemes, which are the successors of assistance schemes, the State finances through taxation (fully or to a large extent) a system of uniform benefits for the benefit of all the residents in the country. Numerous countries which had previously adopted this model of benefits have moved back to the principle of social assistance, and now allocate a full or partial pension only on a means-tested basis.

It should be added that, even in those countries in which the system is based primarily on social insurance, there may be a form of social assistance for persons who do not come within the scope of the main scheme or who receive insurance benefits which are not sufficient to cover their needs.

On the other hand, in some countries with a universal non-contributory pension scheme, supplements to the base amounts may be payable on a means-tested basis.

Provident funds

In some developing countries, in Asia, Africa and the Pacific, legislation provides for the protection of workers by means of "national provident funds" (which cover the risks of old-age, invalidity and loss of the family breadwinner). As a general rule these funds, which are financed by employer and employee contributions and administered by the State, pay a lump sum to the beneficiary who has reached a stipulated age and fulfills certain conditions. This amount is, in most cases, equal to the sum of the contributions paid, increased by the accrued interest that has been added to the employee's account. In certain countries, there is provision for transforming the lump sum into an annuity. With this reserve in mind, provident funds do not guarantee (as required by ILO international labour standards on old-age, invalidity and survivor benefits) the payment of benefits in the form of periodic payments. Moreover, there is no pooling of risks among participants, as is the case with social insurance. In this respect, the system of provident funds, with benefits based on each participant's individual account, is close to the mandatory retirement savings schemes established in some Latin American countries, in particular Chile.

It is often considered that these systems form a first step towards more comprehensive protection of workers by the introduction of pension insurance schemes. Indeed, national provident funds have been converted into pension schemes in many countries, in particular in the Caribbean and the Near East. Nevertheless, this second step is often a difficult one to make; there are countries where a conversion of this type has been under study for many 20 years (such as Sri Lanka and Indonesia).

---

*Throughout this manual, reference is made to and information provided on the pension schemes of several countries. That information is taken from *Social Security Programs Throughout the World - 1995*. Social Security Administration, Office of Research and Statistics. Washington DC. USA.
[SSA Publication No. 13-11805. July 1995. (Research Report #64)].

C. Combined methods of protection

In a significant number of countries, the legislation brings together two systems: one which provides basic uniform pensions for all persons; the other providing earnings-related benefits for all or nearly all employees, or for all workers, employees and self-employed persons.

Earnings related schemes provide an additional level of protection. Two-tier or three-tier systems (the third tier being that of individual insurance) develop according to very different patterns. In many countries in Europe and Africa, the same public scheme ensures both basic protection and earnings related protection (for example Finland, Israel, Jamaica, Japan, Latvia, Norway, Poland, Switzeland).

Fig. 2:
"The two and three tier systems ..."

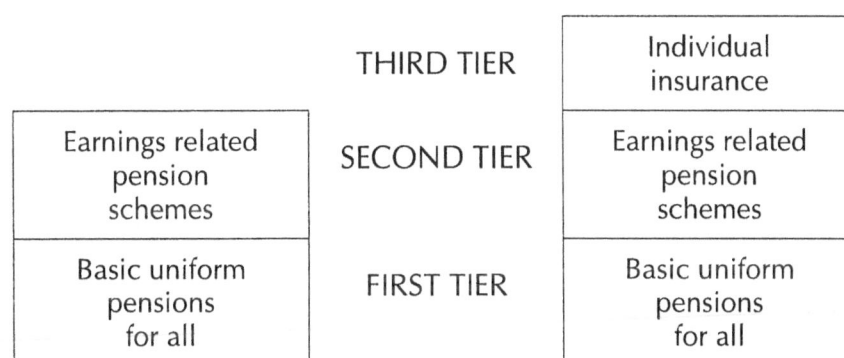

	THIRD TIER	Individual insurance
Earnings related pension schemes	SECOND TIER	Earnings related pension schemes
Basic uniform pensions for all	FIRST TIER	Basic uniform pensions for all

Single or multiple schemes

Before the introduction of pension insurance schemes applicable to relatively large categories of employees, there existed in many countries special schemes covering limited occupational groups, such as military personnel, civil servants, miners, seafarers or railway workers. These schemes often existed alongside a general scheme covering a large proportion of wage-earners, with their members being exempt from membership of the general scheme.

The special schemes provide conditions which are equal to, or frequently more favourable than, those of the general scheme in the area of pension entitlement (for example, a lower pensionable age) and in the calculation of the pension amount.

In certain European and Latin American countries, there have been or still are very many special schemes, some of which cover only a small category of workers. The categories of beneficiaries may be very disparate: in one country, these are forest workers; in another, for example, the clerks of public notaries, the employees of the Central Bank or opera dancers.

In contrast to special schemes for employees, the conditions under the more recently established special schemes for self-employed persons may be less favourable where these have not wished to be integrated into the general scheme, in particular since they fear that an excessively heavy financial burden will be placed on them. Similarly, where a distinction has been made between agricultural wage-earners and other wage-earners, the scheme applicable to the former has, at least at the outset, proved less generous (for example, in Turkey).

In many countries, there has been progress towards unification of the schemes. Either the special schemes for some groups of employees, or some of these schemes, have been integrated into the general scheme; however, the integration into the basic scheme may have been accompanied by the establishment of a complementary special scheme. This has particularly been the case for civil servants in many countries. On the other hand, there are countries where certain self-employed persons have been grouped together with salaried employees. In one country, several categories of self-employed persons have been integrated into a large scheme covering all non-wage-earning persons. A third possibility has been that of setting up a basic scheme covering all residents, which is usually a non-contributory pension scheme. In several countries, a contributory scheme applying the principles of insurance has been made compulsory for the population as a whole (national insurance scheme).

D. Extension of protection

Over the years, social protection in general, and social security for old-age in particular, has been extended to an increasingly large number of categories of persons. In certain countries, entitlement to an old-age pension has become universal (for example Canada, Denmank, Hong Kong, Iceland, Mauritius). Nonetheless, the Beveridge* objective of extending cover to the population as a whole continues to be a serious challenge for many countries.

Widening the scope of application

In general, community intervention to the benefit of the elderly initially covered specific categories of the population. At the outset, assistance measures were intended to relieve the distress of the least well-off sectors of the population at a time when destitution was widespread, particularly amongst the elderly. Subsequently, this intervention was aimed at particular socio-professional groups which were the object of special interest on the part of the public authorities, such as military personnel, civil servants and seafarers.

---

* Beveridge, Sir William. 1942. *Social Insurance and Allied Services.* London, England: H.M. Stationey Office.

The growth of industrialization, and consequently of the wage-earning population, increased the number of wage-earners living at subsistence level and incapable of making a voluntary effort to save from their income the amounts needed to enable them to live after the end of their working life. In this way the first compulsory insurance schemes developed, based on contributions from wage-earners and employers (in many cases together with a contribution from the community) so as to provide elderly workers with a means of subsistence.

These schemes usually affected only industrial and commercial employees, to the exclusion of agricultural wage-earners and, even at the beginning, only those whose incomes did not exceed the level above which it was thought possible to make a voluntary savings effort, i.e. the membership ceiling.

For administrative and financial reasons, in some Latin American and Asian countries, protection was limited at the start not only to certain categories of employees but also to certain geographical regions.

Gradually, the system was extended everywhere and coverage was also extended to exclude particular categories of wage-earners: agricultural workers, domestic personnel, workers receiving a high wage (with a benefit ceiling replacing a membership ceiling) and, under certain legislations, those employed by small enterprises. Currently, pension schemes cover all employees in the most industrialized countries. However, there are still some exceptions, even in those countries.

Going beyond the framework of work for wages or salaries, after the Second World War numerous countries brought into the circle of protected persons all or part of the self-employed, either into the same scheme as wage-earners or by setting up one or more special schemes. Various countries have extended protection to very different categories such as artists, writers, students, members of religious communities, and categories of persons doing jobs similar to that of employees, such as apprentices and trainees, domestic personnel and so on.

In developing countries, the situation is much more diversified. In some countries coverage continues to extend only to civil servants. The majority of countries base their decisions concerning the scope of pension schemes on the existence of an employer-employee relationship. The legislation applies to workers with such a relationship or to those who are providing their services under an employment contract. For example, legislation in the French-speaking African countries, which applies to all "wage-earners", refers back to the Labour Code for a definition of this term.

Many national legislations continue to exclude various categories of employees: those whose wages are lower than a specified minimum or whose wages exceed a given amount; agricultural workers; domestic employees; wage-earners in small enterprises and casual, temporary or seasonal workers. Even where the legislation does not specifically exclude certain categories of workers, the difficulties inherent in defining the term "employee" may present themselves in the case of persons who have been engaged on the basis of a sub-contract.

Progress in expanding coverage of schemes is certainly less rapid in developing countries than in industrialized countries. Nevertheless, compulsory protection is gradually spreading. Excluded categories may also be reduced. For example, several countries have lowered the minimum number of workers required for bringing an enterprise into the scope of the scheme, for example from 100 to 20 workers. Furthermore, certain developing countries have also widened the coverage of pension protection to some or all self-employed workers.

The purpose of universal coverage

·One of the principles of social security coming out of the Beveridge Report and the ILO Income Security Recommendation, 1944 (No. 67), is that of universal coverage: protection should be extended to the national community as a whole. Social security is not the aspiration of only one social class, certain professional categories or underprivileged groups; it should meet the needs of all workers and, as a human right, those of all the population.

It is therefore a question of eliminating inequalities between social or occupational groups and of establishing general solidarity on the part of the community, for the benefit of all residents. The tendency in industrialized countries is to widen coverage and to make protection universally available, even though the ultimate objective of this doctrine has not yet been attained everywhere. In developing countries, extension of coverage is an objective which is difficult to achieve.

Fig. 3:
"... Universal coverage ..."

Industrialized countries

In those countries which introduced non-contributory pension schemes for all residents, protection was made available for all, right from the start. The same applies in countries which instituted "national insurance schemes," contributory schemes applicable to the population as a whole.

It has been seen that, in other countries, progressive extension has often made it possible to cover virtually all the employed. However, in many cases, this has only been done by maintaining inequalities in the level of protection afforded. Nevertheless there still continues to be people who slip through the net of protection based on occupational categories. In particular, over the past 15 years, developments in new forms of work and employment have brought with them new categories of atypical workers poorly suited to occupational-based schemes. Similarly, the growth in categories without work and marginalized calls for the implementation of special measures to guarantee their means of existence, in particular in old age. It is not certain that personal insurance which has been introduced in many countries, offering everybody who does not have compulsory coverage the possibility of voluntary membership, will be sufficient in this respect. The institution of non-contributory schemes linked to residence, which address these underprivileged categories, seems to be essential.

Developing countries

In developing countries, extending pension protection to categories such as agricultural workers or self-employed persons may raise some very difficult problems. For example, the difficulty of extending protection to agricultural wage-earners lies in organizing, administering and financing the schemes. The labour force is often unstable, seasonal, scattered over vast areas and incomes are low. Moreover, it may be difficult to distinguish between agricultural wage-earners and other categories of agricultural workers.

Protecting self-employed workers may also raise difficulties in these conditions. The non-wage-earning populations are usually extremely diverse, both in rural and urban areas. Many belong to the informal sector of the economy. In various countries, the elderly, disabled and survivors are traditionally taken care of by the extended family but extended families are now less and less common. It has been found that difficult periods of shortages affect the elderly in particular. However, providing them with reasonable periodic benefits runs into obstacles: they often have no contributory capacity during their working life and there is no external and adequately broad economic base for social solidarity to come into play.

In spite of these considerable difficulties, more or less pronounced depending on the country, a certain number have attempted to progress towards universal coverage by making use of innovative forms of protection.

UNIT 2: Private Schemes

A. Relationship between private and public schemes

Public pension schemes have developed remarkably for around a century and especially over the past 50 years. This progressive extension of public protection has not, however, prevented the development of private protection. Currently, private schemes are widely found in many countries, both developing and industrialized. Their number and importance have grown considerably since the 1950's in many countries.

The institution of a private scheme may be the outcome of an employer's initiative (a company scheme), collective bargaining (occupational and inter-occupational schemes) or, although rare except in the case of self-employed persons, at the initiative of the workers themselves. In certain countries, the employer-provided schemes are by far the most common, whereas in others those based on collective agreements are more prevalent. There are large differences in type and technique between the private schemes.

The development of private schemes is usually closely linked to the situation of the public schemes. Private schemes may supplement public schemes when the replacement rate is low or when, in Beveridge-type systems, the flat-rate pension is set at a relatively low level. They may target workers with higher than average wages where pensions have a ceiling. In principle, the lower the level of pensions and the pension ceiling, the greater the opportunities for the development of private schemes. Generous fiscal incentives also contribute to their development, as has been seen in several industrialized countries. Private schemes may also be a substitute for public schemes. For example, there are countries where private schemes offer coverage which is at least equal to the public earnings-related pension scheme and where it is possible for a private scheme to replace the public scheme for certain insured persons whose employer "contracts out" of the public scheme (for example Japan, Singapore, Switzerland, United Kingdom).

It should be added that, in countries where public schemes have been introduced only at a late date, private schemes developed long before. This was the case in the developing countries where these schemes had offered, for some time, the only type of pension protection that existed, in a preliminary form.

Chile, in 1981, started an individual account scheme managed by private investment management firms that replaced, for all new workforce entrants, the public scheme. Workers must choose which investment management firm they want to manage their pension fund account. Several other countries in Latin America have since instiuted schemes either of partial or of voluntary replacement of the public scheme with a privately managed scheme.

As a whole, development of public social protection has not held back the expansion of private protection. To a certain extent, the security guaranteed by public schemes has stimulated a need for complementary protection and has opened new possibilities for private initiative. In contrast, however, the existence of private schemes has proved to be a stimulus for the improvement of public schemes which, in several countries, have built up a second, compulsory, layer of protection thus reducing the space left open to the private sector. Today, however, there is a resurgence of interest in private protection and it seems possible that the expansion of private protection will go hand in hand with some degree of contraction in the public schemes in a number of countries.

In many countries there is an established relationship between the public sector and the private sector because all the components of protection are looked at as a whole. The desired total amount for the pension that should be achieved, from adding together the public and private benefits, is established. The schemes are therefore co-ordinated to achieve this purpose. Co-ordination may be closer when there is a guaranteed overall income replacement rate.

The requirements of international labour standards can also be fulfilled by private schemes, under certain conditions, and in conjunction with other forms of protection, where appropriate. The Social Security (Minimum Standards) Convention, 1952 (No. 102), provides that Member states which have ratified the Convention may take account of voluntary insurance schemes if they

(a) are under the supervision of the public authorities or administered jointly by employers and workers;

(b) cover a substantial part of those persons whose earnings are below a specified level (those of a skilled manual male employee); and

(c) comply with the other relevant provisions of the Convention with regard to qualifying conditions, benefit levels and so on. These same provisions are also included in the Invalidity, Old-Age and Survivors' Benefits Convention, 1967 (No. 128).

B. Advantages and disadvantages of private schemes

The interests of the private schemes may conflict with those of the public schemes in the allocation of financial resources, i.e. the contributions paid by insured persons and/or employers. Discussions on the role of private schemes are currently a priority in many countries. Often they go beyond the framework of technical considerations and raise questions of ideology and, in particular, the role that should be played by the State.

Nevertheless, from an objective viewpoint, the following advantages may be listed:

- The existence and the development of private schemes opens the way to initiatives on the part of interested groups and allows them to complement, by their own efforts, public protection.

- Private schemes have the flexibility required to meet the special needs of specific enterprises, sectors of activity or occupations.

- They may be more effective than the public schemes in dealing with the demands for benefits, thanks to the incentive of competition.

- If they are not compulsory, private schemes must be financed on a funded basis and, preferably, fully funded. They must therefore accumulate a large volume of funds which can be invested and this may increase savings and make a major contribution to national capital formation.

In contrast, private schemes can be criticized on a number of points, based on the following considerations:

- More often than not, private schemes have a profit motive and they sometimes have high administrative costs, due in particular to promotional expenses. In many countries, it has been found that administrative costs and profits may absorb 35 to 50 per cent of the premiums paid.

- They reduce national solidarity. They very often have a limited scope of coverage and they favour the better-off categories of the population while ignoring the economically worse-off workers. The fiscal incentives from which they often benefit, which are in fact a subsidy from public funds, operate in the same direction.

- Private schemes are exposed to a danger of bankruptcy and, consequently, do not guarantee total security unless the State takes the necessary measures to provide guarantees of solvency.

- Adjusting pensions to economic fluctuations is much more difficult to carry out in private funded schemes than in public pay-as-you-go schemes. In practice it is almost impossible to institute pre-established indexation mechanisms.

- In the event of professional mobility, which leads the worker to change from one private scheme to another, maintenance of pension rights raises complex problems which are difficult to resolve.

C. *The current debate*

Increasingly, the development of private schemes is on the agenda in many countries and, in particular, those in which ssuch schemes were until now of very little significance.

This development forms part of a wider trend towards privatization and is at the same time linked with the financial difficulties confronting the majority of public pension schemes. Their cost is constantly increasing under the impact of several factors. In the first place, the schemes are "maturing," i.e., as the years pass, the number of beneficiaries entitled to a full-rate pension continues to rise. Secondly, population ageing increases pension expenditure and, in the industrial countries, the beginning of the twenty first century will witness a demographic imbalance due to the simultaneous arrival, at working age, of the low birth-rate generation and the arrival, at retirement age, of the baby-boom generation. Finally, the employment situation, on the one hand, transfers to the pension schemes a part of the burden resulting from unemployment and, on the other, produces a fall in the funds available by reducing the number of active contributors and the income from contributions in social insurance schemes. In order to safeguard public pension schemes rigorous measures have been taken in many countries, combined, where necessary, with financing reform.

Nevertheless, there is an important school of thought which considers it essential to redistribute the responsibilities, for income maintenance and guaranteed income (to the elderly in particular) between the public sector and the private sector. More specifically, since the rigorous measures mentioned above would mean a reduction in the income replacement rate of pensions, it will be necessary to compensate this reduction by calling increasingly on the private sector. These ideas, which have been supported by pressure from various interest groups including insurance companies and banks, underlie many pieces of legislation recently adopted with a view to stimulating the private pension sector.

A World Bank report, **Averting the Old Age Crisis**, goes further in this direction by recommending that the role of public schemes be limited to the payment of modest pensions, if possible only to the least well-off elderly, and to entrust private commercial pension funds with compulsory retirement pensions. According to the report, such an approach, as it is based on funded schemes, could respond to the ageing crisis and stimulate economic growth. The approach is derived from what is called the "Chilean model."

Fig. 4:
"The current debate ..."

D. The "Chilean model"

In 1980-81, the pension system in Chile was reformed under the military regime. This gave rise to a new type of scheme: the privately-managed mandatory retirement savings scheme (MRS). The existing public pension scheme, which had provided earnings-related pensions and which was financed out of current income (pay-as-you-go), was replaced – except in the case of long-term insured persons who opted to remain in the old scheme – by participation in retirement savings plans administered by competing commercial firms chosen by the insured persons. Employers no longer pay any contributions, since the new system is financed entirely by workers' contributions which are paid into their individual accounts. The amount of the pension depends on the contributions paid by the participant and the interest credited to his or her account. The role of the State is limited to setting the rules, supervising of the funds and guaranteeing minimum pensions. Public social security has thus been reduced to guaranteeing minimum pensions, supplemented by a compulsory private scheme of savings accumulation.

This reform has been the inspiration of new legislation adopted in some other Latin American countries. However, to date, it has not had any decisive influence elsewhere in the world. It may be that proposals of this type will be difficult to accept in many countries since such radical changes would not generate the political consensus needed for their adoption, in particular if they are perceived as a regression in social protection.

PENSION SCHEMES

MODULE 2:
OLD-AGE BENEFITS

International Labour Office - Geneva

MODULE CONTENTS

MODULE 2

OLD-AGE BENEFITS

UNIT 1: Pensionable age

A. General outline

All societies must address the question of how to look after the elderly. Traditionally, the family and the community took this responsibility and continue to do so to varying degrees today. Starting from the end of the nineteenth century, several countries took measures to establish a system of old-age protection. Currently, as a result of the considerable progress achieved since the Second World War, there are few countries in which there is no social protection for the elderly.

The common objective of old-age protection schemes is to guarantee income security to the elderly, by means of the payment of cash benefits intended to form the major part, if not the totality, of their income.

Virtually throughout the world, old-age pension schemes are the modern method used to maintain the standard of living of the elderly. Old-age pensions are the most important of all social security benefits, not only from the economic and financial point of view but also from the psychological and political point of view. It is therefore useful to examine these schemes in detail. In addition, many of the provisions are applicable to invalidity and survivors' benefits, which are usually linked to old-age pension schemes.

As a general rule, national legislation lays down the minimum age at which an old-age pension is normally paid. However, in some cases it is stipulated that a pension can be granted without age requirements in the event of long-term service. The minimum pensionable age is not necessarily the same for everyone. Distinctions may be made to allow for differences in situations from one person to another. In particular, the age may vary depending on sex, occupation or the arduous nature or duration of the work that has been done during a person's working life.

Yet at the same time, there is a trend to a more flexible approach to the rules governing pensionable age, in different cases and under different circumstances. First, however, a clear distinction should be made between pensionable age and retirement age, which are two different concepts even though they may overlap.

B. Pensionable age and retirement age

Pensionable age is the minimum age at which an insured person fulfills the conditions for obtaining a normal old-age pension. **Retirement age** is the age at which a worker ceases gainful, regular and substantial employment as the result of advanced age. These two may be linked in law if giving up gainful employment is a condition for pension entitlement, which is often the case for the payment of non-contributory pensions and may also be found in some social insurance schemes.

Social insurance legislation in many countries, however, does not stipulate that payment of an old-age pension requires cessation of gainful employment. The rationale is that the worker acquires the right to an old-age pension by paying contributions over a certain period of time and, consequently, the pension has to be paid when the stipulated age has been reached, whether or not the insured person continues in gainful employment.

Even though they may not be linked in law, the two aspects – cessation of occupational activity and pension entitlement – remain complementary. The worker's decision to claim a pension is influenced by the possibility of receiving a pension which guarantees an adequate substitute income and, on the other hand, the decision taken by the enterprise to retire him or her is easier when there is an old-age pension scheme. In this way, the setting of pensionable age is the key factor which most often influences *actual* retirement. Nevertheless, these two aspects may be considered separately: retirement may take place before or after pensionable age, even though it is, to a relatively large extent, dependent on the conditions in the labour market.

C. Normal pensionable age

Setting a pensionable age

There are several reasons behind the setting of a pensionable age. It may be considered that, once a certain age is achieved, the worker is entitled to enjoy a justified rest in compensation for the efforts, achievements and contributions that have been made during the course of a working life. Historically, the first pensions granted, often on a discretionary basis to civil servants and military staff, derive from this concept of compensation for services rendered and the right to rest. It has also been presumed that, at a certain age, the worker's physical and mental capacities are reduced so that it would no longer be equitable to force him or her to continue in occupational activities.

Based on the assumption that advanced age is accompanied by disability, this was the concept lying behind the first pension insurance scheme. The German Act of 1889, which introduced a compulsory invalidity insurance, provided for pensions to be granted without proof of invalidity as from 70 years of age. It was also adopted by the ILO at the 1944 International Labour Conference. Indeed, according to the Income Security Recommendation (No. 67), 1944, "the contingency for which old-age benefit should be paid is the attainment of a prescribed age, which should be that at which persons commonly become incapable of efficient work, the incidence of sickness and invalidity becomes heavy, and unemployment, if present, is likely to be permanent." It is obvious that these criteria, based on average characteristics of a population and depending on its demographic structure, health status and the working conditions to which elderly workers have been exposed in the past, will vary across countries at different times.

Beyond these considerations, there are other criteria which influence the legislative setting of pensionable age. Demographic considerations (age structure of the population, increase in life expectancy, etc.) play a role. However it is social and, in particular, economic and financial considerations which in the final analysis are often the deciding factors. The cost of financing pensions is of particular importance: the lower the pensionable age, the larger the number of beneficiaries and the higher the cost of the scheme.

A wide range of pensionable ages

Normal pensionable age is usually equal to or lower than 65 years. This age is, moreover, the upper limit laid down in ILO international labour standards, which nevertheless do provide for exceptions. The fact is, however, that the number of countries in which the legal pensionable age is higher than 65 years is at the present time extremely small.

On the whole, pensionable age is higher in industrial countries than in developing countries. In the OECD countries, for example, it is often around 65 years, at least for men. In the large majority of the former centrally planned economy countries, it is 60 years. Many Asian and Latin American countries have also adopted this pensionable age, whereas in African countries and countries with national provident funds, it is frequently lower, for example 55 years. The large divergences between industrial and developing countries in average life expectancy are often put forward to justify these disparities. Nonetheless, it should be noted that, although life expectancy at birth varies considerably, this is to a large extent attributable to the degree of infant mortality. At higher ages – 50 to 60 years – the differences are usually much smaller.

Although pension schemes are subject to relatively frequent changes, the normal pensionable age usually varies little over time. In many countries it has remained unchanged for 50 years or more.

Nevertheless, there has been a trend to lowering pensionable age in some countries where the legal pensionable age had been the highest. This was either to meet the aspirations of workers wishing to take their retirement earlier or because of rising unemployment, which encourages the retirement from employment of elderly workers. In some cases it was for these two reasons together. At the present time there is more of a trend in the opposite direction and this is attributable, in particular, to financial considerations especially in countries in transition to a market economy. However, the planned increase can be undertaken only very progressively.

D. Lowering pensionable age on the basis of specific criteria

Differentiation on grounds of sex

Many countries give women the right to collect old-age benefits at an earlier age than men; the difference is usually five years. The question of different or equal pensionable ages for men and women is very complex and gives rise to considerable discussion. Opinions are divided on the desirability of this difference in treatment. Those who defend a lower pensionable age for women consider, in particular, that women who are in gainful employment continue to carry out a large part of the household chores and family activities, such as education of the children. In addition to the fact that they alone bear the physiological consequences of maternity, they therefore continue to carry a double burden. It is also argued that an earlier pension age responds to women's wishes to collect their pension at the same time as their husbands, who are often older than they. Perhaps a more important reason is that, after a certain age, women have difficulty in finding employment.

Those who recommend the same pensionable age for men and women assert that setting a lower age is not necessarily an advantage for women. It does, in fact, result in a shortening of their occupational career which, together with the lower salaries they often receive, is a handicap for them; consequently, women collect smaller pensions than do men. It is paradoxical that a lower age is set for women despite the fact that, in most countries, their life expectancy is greater than that of men and therefore they can expect to collect their pensions for a longer period of time.

The discrimination between men and women on pensionable age produces considerable criticism and, in some countries, the question of setting the same age is being discussed as part of the application to social security of the general principle of equality of treatment for men and women. Application of this principle does, however, entail practical difficulties. Should the pensionable age for women gradually be raised to the same level as that for men? Should the pensionable age for men be lowered to that currently applied to women? Should one adopt a single age somewhere between the two? The answer will also be influenced by the constraints laid down by the general economic situation and the financial constraints of the pension schemes.

Differentiation by type of work

In many countries, the pensionable age has been lowered for certain categories of workers. There are first the categories of wage-earners for whom the special schemes had been set up before the creation of general pension schemes. Examples are, in the public sector, civil servants and career military personnel and, in the private sector, miners, seafarers and railway workers. These schemes have often continued alongside the general scheme and they conserve special advantages considered to be traditional. Among the advantages is a retirement age which is often five or more years lower than the legal pensionable age.

Furthermore, some national legislations set a lower age for workers who have been long employed on arduous, dangerous or unhealthy work. There is a wide range of provisions on the list of jobs involved and the length of employment considered. In countries in transition, wages are (or were) classified by category depending on the type of work done; the retirement age reduction is respectively ten and five years for the two "privileged" categories. This general classification, however, raises difficulties since what is arduous work today will not necessarily be so in the future due to changes in technology.

Lowering the age in the event of unemployment

The increasing imbalance in the labour market over the past 20 years has led to a number of countries lowering the pensionable age for elderly unemployed persons, in general up to five years before the normal age. A few countries in Europe and Latin America had long since taken similar measures in cases where the unemployment of an older worker seemed likely to be permanent.

Lowering the age in the event of long-term employment

Some countries lower the normal pensionable age for insured persons whose length of insurance far exceeds the normal period. These early pensions are usually called "seniority pensions" and there are no specific age conditions. This is also to the benefit of workers who entered employment at an early age, after the end of their compulsory schooling, who are often also those who have been employed on the most arduous and least gratifying jobs. This practice is costly and is increasingly being called into question.

E.   Flexibility in pensionable age

For some time now there has been a tendency to question the very concept of "normal pensionable age", based on the "average" ageing in a population, in view of the recognition of the differential and progressive nature of individual ageing and people's desire for greater freedom of choice in how they organize their working lives. The process of ageing for individuals, in fact, is extremely varied due in particular to conditions of work and lifestyle. At a given age, health status, attitude to work, interests and so on will vary greatly from one person to another. It has also been found that stopping work from one day to the next, especially when this is not wanted, may have severe psychological consequences for the person in question. Consequently a movement has developed for greater individualization in retirement age. This implies leaving the worker greater latitude in advancing or delaying the age at which an old-age benefit is collected, depending on the individual's abilities and preferences, in effect, "retirement à la carte".

The greater flexibility implied by this trend, however, does have its limits. It would be extremely difficult, for obvious financial and administrative reasons, to take fully into consideration the fact that individuals do age at a different pace and to give individuals free reign to chose their own time of retirement. Consequently, although different forms of increased flexibility have been introduced in a number of countries, the reference to a "normal" pensionable age remains. The early old-age pensions, referred to above, may be considered a way of making retirement age more flexible. This

is also the case for other legal provisions for early pensions, such as provisions for women who have born and raised one or more children, found in several countries.

However, increased individualization of pensionable age is achieved especially when the worker can voluntarily decide to advance or delay his entitlement to old-age pension or when a system of progressive retirement is introduced.

Increased flexibility for personal convenience

Some national legislation gives the insured person the possibility of taking an early retirement on request, as from a stipulated age (frequently set at five years before the normal age) provided minimum requirements regarding periods of insurance have been fulfilled. In such a case, since there is no social justification for early retirement, a reduced benefit is paid, based on the number of years involved. In contrast, in the cases of early retirement looked at above, the insured person collects the pension to which he would have been entitled at normal pensionable age. This reduction compensates, to a certain degree, the advantage granted for mere personal convenience (although the employer may sometimes supplement the pension on the basis of a company agreement) and is intended to ensure that the cost is not borne by the other insured persons. However, the reduction may be calculated in such a way as to encourage, or on the other hand discourage, insured persons from taking up such a provision.

Some systems allow insured persons, should they be able and wish to continue working, to put off their application for an old-age pension beyond the normal age. The amount of pension is then increased by a coefficient proportional to the number of years for which the pension has been postponed. These increases, symmetrical to the reductions for early pensions, make it possible to compensate, to a certain degree, for the reduction in the period for which the pension will be paid. The increase may be relatively generous when a country wishes to encourage workers to remain productive as long as possible. Commonly, postponement of retirement may be authorized without limit of time or be possible only up to a prescribed age (for example, 70 years). It has been found that use of deferred pensions has often been a palliative employed to counter the effect of low pension levels and that any improvement in the level tended to reduce the number of deferments. However, deferred retirement may continue to be attractive if the increases which are offered are high. Obviously, this is feasible only if the employment situation makes it possible for the insured person to continue working.

Progressive retirement

The sharp distinction between full-time work and full retirement is increasingly criticized in view of the stress which may be brought about by suddenly ceasing to work at a specified age. Consequently, in order to avoid the sudden break brought about by retirement, it has long seemed particularly desirable to arrange a transition between full-time work and retirement. In this way, for example, the ILO Older Workers Recommendation (No. 162), 1980, provides for a progressive reduction in hours of work, compensated by the award of a suitable benefit.

Progressive retirement makes it possible to make a less rigid choice between retirement and work. It offers the ageing worker the opportunity of reducing his or her occupational activity for several years before the time for claiming an old-age pension, or perhaps even after this time, since both a lower and an upper limit are fixed. The loss in pay resulting from a reduction in working time is compensated, in part, by the payment of a partial pension. Partial pension schemes offer workers the opportunity of progressively reducing their work load, over their final years of employment. This ensures a smooth transition to retirement without too sharp a reduction in income, since total income (wages plus pension) is only slightly lower than the previous income from full-time work. Of course this progressive approach must be voluntary, leaving a worker with free choice.

This system was introduced in Sweden at the end of the 1970's. It is aimed at wage-earners, salaried employees or self-employed persons aged from 60 to 64 years, who reduce their working time while continuing to work within a weekly range of hours. Insured persons have the opportunity to take advantage of this reduction in several stages. This new scheme has met with a significant success.

Several other European countries have taken similar measures, either statutory or on the basis of collective agreements, although different modalities may be used.

Pre-retirement

A number of countries, as already indicated, have reduced the pensionable age for those older workers who are unemployed. In addition, starting in the 1970's, measures were introduced to encourage older workers (including those still employed) to give up work entirely. This was essentially to promote the employment of young people who, following the post-war demographic boom, were entering the labour market in large numbers. Under these "pre-retirement" programmes older workers, who agree to retire or who are threatened with dismissal, receive a benefit until the age at which they can collect an old-age pension. These programmes have been introduced through collective agreements or by legislation, usually as part of unemployment insurance, but also in the framework of old-age insurance.

To ensure that these measures contribute more directly to the employment of younger unemployed workers, a link has often been established between the early retirement of existing workers and the hiring of new workers. Some programmes make entitlement to early retirement conditional upon the enterprise replacing early retirees by young persons, in equal numbers, in particular by young persons looking for their first job.

In general, these measures have considerably reduced the number of older workers. However, it is not clear that this has always had an effect on the reduction of unemployment among young persons, since the departure of older workers is often accompanied by other changes aimed at increasing productivity. In the long term, these measures are not without severe drawbacks. They may result in a loss of productive capacity and a waste of experience, deprive the retirees of social contacts and create a risk of premature ageing. Furthermore, they lead to a significant increase in social expenditure, which cannot always be justified.

Table 1 provides a comparison of the provisions for statutory pensionable age in a random selection of countries.

Table 1: Pensionable age in selected countries

Country	Men	Women	Early retirement (basis)
Argentina	63	58	(Changing to 65/60 by the year 2001). Retirement age can be lowered for up to 10 years for hazardous/unhealthy work.
Australia	65	60	
Bahamas	65	65	
Bolivia	55	50	50/45 for hazardous occupations
Botswana**	60	60	Age 45
Brazil	65	60	Age 50 if in various types of ardous employment for 15-25 years.
China	60	60	For professional men and women.
		55	for non-professional salaried women.
		50	For other women.
	55	50	For ardous/unhealthy work.
Czech Republic	60		Men 55-58 for ardous/unhealthy work.
		53-57	Women 53-57, depending on number of children raised. By 2007 men will retire at 62, women from 56-61.
Denmark	67	67	50-66 for social and health-related reasons. Age 58-66 if work ability is reduced by at least half (for physical or mental reasons.)
Egypt	60	60	For pensions based on basic wage (and with 10 years of contributions).
	50	50	For pensins based on variable wage (and with 20 years of contributions).
Gabon	55	55	Age 50 if jprematurely aged.
Georgia	60		Men with 25 years of covered employment.
		55	Women with 20 years of work. Both reduced for hazardous/ardous work: for mothers of 4 or more/or handicapped children
Ghana	60	60	Age 55-59, unless ardous work.
Guinea	55	55	Age 50 if unable to work or with 5-10% reduction for each year under 55.
Iran	60	55	50/45 for 20-25 years working in unhealthy regions or occupations.
Italy	62	57	Need 15 years of coverage. Pensionable age increased in 1995 from 61 and 56.
Japan	65	65	Paid at 60-64 with actuarial reduction.
Morocco	60	60	Age 55 for miners with 5 or more years of work underground.

Country	Men	Women	Early retirement (basis)
Tunisia	60	60	Age 50 if prematurely aged because of ardous work, or unemployed for 6 months (360 months of contributions). Age 50 for mother of 3 children (180 months of contributions); Age 50 (360 months of contributions) with 0.5% reductions for each quarter below age 60.
Uganda*	55	55	Age 50 if retired from full-time employment.
United Kingdom	65	60	Between the years 2010 and 2020 it is proposed that the pensionable age for women be raised gradually from 60 to 65.
Vietnam	60	55	55/50 with 20 years of hazardous or unhealthy work or with 10 years of work in South Vietnam, Laos or Kampuchea before 1975.
Zimbabwe	60	60	Age 55 if ardous work.

*   Provident fund
**   Public employees only

Source: U.S. Social Security Administration, *Social security programs throughout the world — 1995,* Washington, D.C., 1995.

UNIT 2: Type, calculation and level of benefits

A. Lump-sum payments

Old-age benefits usually take the form of periodic payments (pensions); however, in certain schemes or in certain cases, they are payable in the form of a lump sum. This feature will be dealt with before looking at the various formulae for calculating pensions.

Although, according to ILO instruments (Conventions Nos. 102 and 128), old-age benefits should be in the form of periodic payments, national provident funds usually make a single lump-sum payment. The same applies to some complementary private schemes in various countries. There are also several schemes which pay out a lump sum when the insured person does not meet the conditions required for allocation of a pension, as will be pointed out in the section on pension calculation.

National provident funds

National provident funds provide for payment at specified ages of a lump sum equal to the cumulative amount of contributions paid by the insured person and his or her employer, together with accumulated interest. Consequently there is no group pooling of risk. Some legislations stipulate that the capital may be used to purchase an annuity although, so far, this practice has been little applied. In very rare cases, social insurance schemes also make a lump-sum payment.

Some people consider that the payment of a lump-sum benefit may be a procedure which is well adapted to needs in developing countries; for example, where an urban wage-earner uses this capital to set up an economic activity in the rural environment of his origin after retirement. However, experience shows that there is a significant danger that the capital will be used for current consumption and it therefore provides the retired person with assistance far below what might have been expected from payment of a periodic benefit. Consequently, it is generally considered that the lump sum paid out by provident funds is very unlikely to meet the ongoing needs of beneficiaries when they retiree and makes only a partial contribution to guaranteeing income for their remaining years. This is all the more so since the capital paid out often loses its real value on account of inflation.

Private pension schemes

It should be noted that, in spite of their name, an increasing number of so-called "pension" schemes in fact pay out a lump-sum benefit, *not* a pension. As with the case of provident funds, although with less severe consequences when a private scheme supplements a public scheme which pays out pensions, this lump sum may be spent as soon as it is received, and it cannot therefore be considered as assuring economic security in old age.

B. Different methods of calculating pensions

As far as pension calculations are concerned, two main types of formulae are found in national legislations (and sometimes they are combined) depending on the concept of the role of old-age pensions. With the first type of formula, everyone who meets the required conditions (age and, often, length of residence in the country) receives a pension at an equal and uniform rate, no matter what the wages or earnings were during the course of the person's occupational career. With the second, the pension amount is calculated on the basis of the insured person's occupational career: it is therefore linked to wages and earnings and it takes into account the length of the beneficiary's career.

Fig. 5:

"... different methods of calculating pensions"

In the first case, the concept is that the community must limit itself to guaranteeing all the elderly a decent minimum existence and, at least, keep them from destitution. The type of formula is derived from the concept of assistance. However, the means-testing implied by this concept has usually been done away with except for the granting of various special supplements linked to the basic pension.

In contrast, the second type of formula is used in social insurance. It accepts that *real* protection of the elderly presupposes maintenance of a standard of living related to that which the insured person enjoyed before retirement and that it is therefore necessary, in all cases, to avoid an excessive fall in this standard of living. To some extent this formula is also consistent with the concept of a pension which, in some way, offers remuneration for past services.

An intermediate formula, falling somewhere between the two described, determines the amount of the pension according to the length of insurance but without taking into account the wages and the earnings of the insured person. Application of this type of formula is limited.

In fact, there is a convergent trend to be seen in many legislations. In countries which had adopted a flat-rate benefit formula, the desire for a retirement income comparable to the income whilst working has encouraged complementary efforts. This has often involved collective solidarity and resulted in the addition of a second level of protection. In these complementary schemes, occupational income is generally taken into account when calculating pensions in the same way as in those countries which established an earnings-related pension right from the beginning.

These latter countries, in their concern to guarantee the most modest pensioners with a decent amount of benefit, have often introduced minimum pensions and instituted (e.g. for those with an incomplete career) non-contributory benefits, which are subject to means testing.

The outcomes of these trends are therefore very similar to each other in the different cases. It makes it possible to increase the effectiveness of protection for the elderly by guaranteeing everybody a decent minimum of existence; taking into account their resources and, for those who have a record of employment, maintenance of a percentage of their previous occupational income.

C. Uniform-rate pensions

Uniform-rate pensions are those paid in schemes which are applicable to all residents. Such schemes are most often non-contributory. However, some social insurance schemes *also* pay flat-rate pensions. It may also happen that the same scheme will pay a pension made up of a flat-rate base amount and an earnings-related component. This is often referred to as a two-tier benefit formula.

It should also be pointed out that "flat-rate" amounts can be subjected to reductions or increases. This applies in particular to schemes (few in number at present) which impose means testing either to all elderly persons or to those who have not yet reached a prescribed age (for example 70 years). More often, means testing will apply only to any pension supplements which are added to the minimum benefits.

In most cases, the pension is payable when the beneficiary has met the minimum eligibility conditions. These usually include a period of residence and in some schemes it is a long period of residence, for example 40 or 50 years, in order to receive a full pension. In those insurance schemes paying flat-rate pensions, a reduction in the normal amount may be stipulated for any insured person who has not had a full occupational career in the insurance scheme. The benefit may be set at a uniform rate for all who are entitled. However in general, a distinction is made between the amount of old-age pension payable to a single person and the amount payable to a married couple (this amount is usually less than twice the amount payable to a single person).

Finally, the pension rate may vary considerably from country to country. In some countries it is still below the subsistence threshold whereas, in others, benefit levels are at or exceed this level. In at least one country the flat-rate pension amount is increased if the beneficiary is not entitled to a complementary pension.

D. Non-earnings-related pensions which vary with the period of insurance

One of the formulae used for determining the amount of a pension is to calculate this amount solely in relation to the length of insurance, without taking into account the insured person's wages or earnings. As has already been pointed out, this is a half-way house between the flat-rate and the earnings-related amounts, although it is closer to the flat-rate pension system, especially where it provides for a reduction in the normal rate if the insured career is incomplete. It is rare for this formula to be applied in statutory pension schemes.

E. Earnings-related pensions

Earnings-related pension schemes are not widely encountered throughout the world, either in developing countries, industrialized countries with market economies or economies in transition.

Qualifying period

In the same way as for flat-rate pensions, the award of benefits is subject to a minimum qualifying period in the majority of earnings-related pension schemes. The stipulated qualifying period is usually dependent on periods of contribution, insurance or employment.

Although certain countries do not stipulate a minimum qualifying period in order to obtain benefit entitlement, the majority of old-age insurance legislations provide that pension entitlement, even at a reduced rate, is dependent on a minimum qualifying period. This qualifying period can be short but, in most cases, it is a long period so as to avoid abuse on the part of those who would contribute merely to exploit the system. In many countries, this period may be as long as 20 years although, under ILO Conventions (Nos. 102 and 128), a reduced benefit must be guaranteed for persons who have completed 15 years of contributions or employment. Some schemes stipulate that the beneficiary must demonstrate that he or she has been registered for at least 20 years, with a certain number of months of insurance during a stipulated period, preceding the date of pension entitlement.

The majority of schemes specify a single qualifying period linked to a single age of pension entitlement. Nevertheless, there are some which stipulate a number of entitlement ages relating to different qualifying periods, the highest ages being linked to the shortest qualifying periods.

Some systems stipulate a certain regularity of contributions. Others may specify that the qualifying period must be completed during a stipulated period immediately preceding the age of pension entitlement. The minimum qualifying period may be reduced in systems in which the pensionable age for certain categories of beneficiaries is lower than the normal age, e.g. women or persons who have been doing work considered to be arduous or unhealthy.

In many countries, periods other than those of employment may be taken into account in making up the minimum qualifying period (and also for pension calculation, as will be seen below). These are known as "assimilated" periods. For example: periods during which the insured person has received social security benefits for sickness, employment injury, maternity, unemployment; periods of compulsory military service; study or training periods; periods devoted to bringing up children and so on.

In countries where there are several pension schemes, many legislations allow insured persons to take into account all periods of insurance acquired under different schemes for calculating the qualifying period.

Since the institution of a relatively long qualifying period will exclude from protection those who are close to pensionable age at the time that the old-age pension scheme is introduced, transition measures are often designed in their favour. For example, the length of the qualifying period may be graduated in relation to age at the time the scheme comes into force, or periods of employment or occupational activity, (real or presumed) which preceded the establishment of the scheme are counted as periods of insurance.

Insured persons who do not fulfill the qualifying conditions often receive a single allowance which may also be calculated in relation to their earnings and number of years of insurance.

Calculation formulae

The amount of an earnings-related pension is usually based on two key factors: the average reference earnings and the length of insurance. These two factors are dealt with in greater detail below and the following paragraphs are devoted to the method of calculation.

The formulae for calculating earnings-related pensions are extremely varied. Nonetheless, a distinction may be made between two major types of formulae, each of which has a number of variants. In the first type, the relation between the pension and previous earnings does not vary in relation to the level of earnings; instead, it usually varies according to the length of insurance or of employment. This is the most widely encountered method of calculation. In some countries which apply this method, the pension amount is calculated as a predetermined percentage of the earnings for each year of insurance or employment. This percentage often ranges between 1.33 and 2 per cent. In this way, an accumulation rate is attributed to each year of insurance and the pension amount is calculated using the following formula:

$$\boxed{\text{Pension}} = \boxed{\text{reference earnings}} \times \boxed{\text{accumulation rate}} \times \boxed{\text{number of years of insurance}}$$

In other countries, the pension is comprised of a base amount (a given percentage of the reference earnings) which is acquired as soon as the minimum qualifying period has been completed and an increment (calculated as a percentage of earnings) for any additional periods of insurance.

In yet other countries, the pension is based on a fixed percentage of the reference earnings if the qualifying period is sufficiently long to make it possible to obtain a full pension (for example, 40 or 45 years). The pension is reduced proportionately when the qualifying period is not complete.

The second type of formula favours those beneficiaries with low earnings, i.e., where the pension is a percentage of previous earnings and where that percentage decreases as the amount of previous earnings increases. There are countries where the pension is calculated on a degressive schedule. The reference earnings are divided into bands and the percentage accounted for by the pension is much greater for the first band than it is for the last. In other countries, the pension is made up of a fixed basic amount – not related to earnings – and to this is added a supplement which is proportional to earnings and to the period of insurance. More complex methods are also used in order to guarantee a pension in which the rate decreases as the reference earnings increase.

Alongside these two calculation formulae may also be found a more innovative method called the "points" method. This is used in several countries although in different ways. For example, in some French-speaking African countries, each year the insured person acquires a number of points calculated on the basis of the amount of contributions paid. The old-age pension is equal to the number of points acquired by the insured person at the time at which his or her benefit is claimed, multiplied by the value of the pension point. The value of the point, whether a contribution point or a pension point, is specified each year by the competent authority using the technical and financial data laid down in the scheme.

Reference earnings and period

The reference wage and earnings used for calculating a pension form one of the key factors influencing the pension level. The reference earnings will depend, on the one hand, on the various earnings components taken into consideration and, on the other hand, on the period taken into account.

The definition of earnings varies from one country to another. In some countries the definition is very broad and covers all wage components, including supplements paid for overtime, allowances, bonuses, benefits in kind, and so on; in others, only the fixed part of the wage paid at regular intervals is taken into account.

Most schemes set an upper limit referred to as a ceiling to the amount of wages or earnings which may be considered when calculating the pension amount. Wages or earnings beyond this ceiling are not taken into consideration. Very often, this ceiling is set as a fixed amount. However, in certain cases, it is calculated by reference to another amount, such as the minimum wage. Instead of applying a ceiling for earnings taken into consideration, some legislations explicitly specify the maximum pension amount. The variations in the level of the ceiling from one country to another – in comparison with GDP per capita, average wage or minimum wage – are considerable. This is due to the fact that, in each country, the level of the ceiling considered suitable is related to economic, financial and social considerations and reflects the interests of different groups. It should also be noted that, in certain schemes, a "floor" has been set, i.e. the amount of earnings taken into consideration cannot be lower than a prescribed minimum.

The system of "wage classes", each class being made up of a minimum and maximum amount, in which the earnings of insured persons are distributed, was widespread in the earliest social insurance schemes. It has been abandoned in most countries but still exists in some, particularly in developing countries. In this system, the reference earnings are not the insured person's *actual* wage, but the *average* wage of the class to which he or she belongs. If the number of classes is very large, the actual wage is close to the average wage for the class.

For the purposes of pension insurance, the earnings of self-employed persons may be those which are defined by income tax legislation. However, many other very different solutions may also be applied. For example, in some developing countries, self-employed workers are classified according to a scale of flat-rate earnings or may select the flat-rate amounts that they wish. Alternatively, the flat-rate amount may be the same for all.

The pension amount is usually calculated from earnings over a reference period, the length of which varies appreciably from one scheme to another. In many schemes, the reference period relates to the entire duration of insurance or to the occupational career of the person in question, or nearly so. In some schemes, the least favourable years are excluded from the calculation. In yet others, however, the length of time taken into consideration is shortened. In certain schemes, this period of time is the final years of insurance or employment (usually from one to ten years). The average reference wage may also be calculated on the "most favourable" years. Sometimes these years have to be consecutive or included in a prescribed period.

Many legislations stipulate an alternative for calculating the period taken into consideration, either by specifying that the most favourable solution should be applied or by leaving the choice of the applicable method to the beneficiary.

When the reference period is of long duration or when this period is far back in time, there is a danger that the nominal earnings recorded for the most distant periods no longer correspond to the range of earnings prevalent at the time at which the pension is being claimed. To deal with this problem, many countries have taken measures to re-value the earnings taken into consideration for pension calculation.

Periods of insurance

The other important factor, in most of the formulae used for calculating pension amounts, is the total length of insurance or employment periods. As mentioned above, a period of insurance is that for which contributions have been paid or is a period of employment. Many legislations assimilate other periods to periods of contribution.

In many schemes, the number of years of insurance that can be taken into consideration for calculating a pension amount is limited. Thus periods of insurance beyond this maximum do not give entitlement to an increase in the pension, even though contributions were paid for these periods. There are schemes where the excess periods may be taken into account but only for calculating the average reference earnings. The maximum period of insurance varies from one scheme to another but is usually between 30 and 45 years. In some schemes the period differs according to the sex of the insured person. In these cases, for equal reference earnings, women will therefore obtain the same pension amount with fewer years of insurance.

Minimum pensions

Pension formulae are often drawn up in such a way as to ensure a minimum amount for beneficiaries. This minimum may be set in different ways. In schemes which have a "floor" for the earnings taken into consideration for pension calculation, the pension will automatically be calculated on the basis of this minimum when the reference earnings are lower than the floor. Many schemes stipulate a fixed minimum amount which may be established according to another reference amount. For example, in many Latin American and French-speaking African countries, it is calculated as a percentage of the minimum wage. As a general rule, the amount of the minimum pension should be set so as to ensure that a pensioner receives a minimum subsistence income.

F. *Pensioners who continue gainful employment*

The provisions concerning the receipt of an old-age pension in combination with the income from gainful employment vary considerably from one country to another and even from one scheme to another in a given country. Many legislations completely forbid such cumulation. Others accept full cumulation without any restriction. Still others, while accepting that it occurs, subject benefits to a prescribed ceiling in relation to earnings and/or the amount of the pension, with the pension being reduced or suspended in consequence. Finally, there are schemes which require cessation of gainful employment up to a prescribed age, after which the protected person may collect a pension without any such restriction on employment or earnings.

Views differ considerably on the subject of cumulation. It may be considered that continuing work is an essential means of preventing acceleration of the ageing process, and should therefore not be discouraged. Alternatively, it is argued that, since the pension is intended to compensate for loss of earnings from employment, the pension should be reduced or suspended, fully or in part, when the insured person does not really need it because he or she continues to receive an income. This is the solution frequently adopted in schemes which provide non-contributory pensions, i.e., those which require no contributions by the covered persons. It is more difficult to adopt the same principle when the insured persons have been required to pay contributions, throughout their working lives, in return for a pension which is to be paid to them at a later date.

The question of accumulating an old-age pension and employment has become more acute in certain countries with the rise in unemployment. It is argued that old-age pension beneficiaries should be discouraged from pursuing or resuming gainful employment in order to free up jobs. However, one may find that many countries suffering from major structural unemployment authorize cumulation without limit, except where pensions are granted before normal pensionable age. The evidence is equivocal. One country that removed the so-called "retirement" test on pensioners found no effect on their labour force participation. Moreover, the right to work is a basic human right and even indirect breaches of this right are open to criticism.

UNIT 3: Maintaining the value of the pension

A. Adjusting pensions in the light of economic fluctuations

Before 1945, pension insurance schemes were organized under the implicit assumption that the national currency would maintain its real value. Nevertheless, in many European countries, currencies collapsed after the First World War. This, however, was considered an exceptional phenomenon due to the consequences of the war. In general, appropriate measures were taken only when the rise in the cost of living was significant. However, as early as 1933 a Danish Act made provision for automatic adjustments.

After the Second World War, the situation changed radically. In accordance with the principles of social security, accepted by virtually all countries, the legal guarantee represented by benefit entitlement had to be supplemented by an economic guarantee so that the benefits, once granted, maintained their real value. Subsequently, the principle of safeguarding the real value of pensions has developed and been turned into a more general principle: maintaining the relationship between a standard of living for pensioners and that of the working population, so that pensioners participate in general prosperity.

With this end in view, adjustment mechanisms were instituted in many countries. They took on a special importance during the periods of inflation which accompanied the years of prosperity in the market economy industrialized countries. Mechanisms of the same type have been set up in many developing countries. However, they have been used in a more irregular way and have therefore been of variable effectiveness. In the former centrally planned economy countries, they have taken on importance only since the liberalization of their economies.

The problem of benefit adjustment is much more complex and more difficult to solve in private funded pension schemes; in particular, those which have been established on the basis of defined contributions.

The adjustment must apply both to past wages being used as the basis for pension calculation (the nominal value of which is eroded yearly, which has an impact on average wages where they are calculated on wages over several years, as in the majority of schemes) and to pensions currently being paid.

There are various methods for adjustment or indexing which may be employed. In many schemes, in particular those applying austerity measures, these methods often come under review in an effort to re-establish financial equilibrium in the schemes.

B. Techniques for adjusting pensions to economic changes

It is possible to identify three main methods of adjustment. The first is systematic, or automatic, adjustment. Under this method the law specifies the procedure, the mechanism and the degree of adjustment. The second method is adjustment which derives from general principles laid out in the law, which itself does not specify either a mechanism or a degree of adjustment. The third is ad hoc adjustment, dictated by circumstances. The law contains no provisions on adjustment.

Fig. 6:

" It is possible to identify three main methods of adjustment "

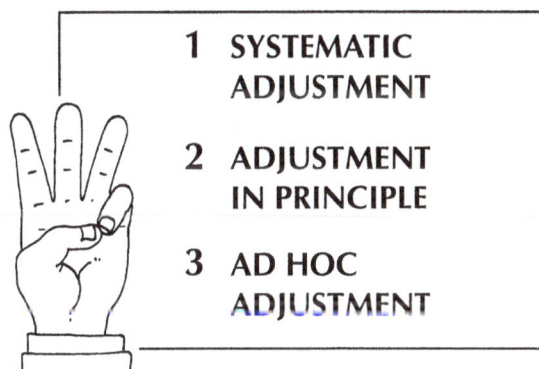

1 SYSTEMATIC ADJUSTMENT

2 ADJUSTMENT IN PRINCIPLE

3 AD HOC ADJUSTMENT

Systematic adjustment

This is an adjustment method which has undergone considerable development since the Second World War. It is the method used in the vast majority of industrial countries and in a number of developing countries. Those legislations which have selected this method always stipulate the standard used for determining the adjustment. In this way, the degree of adjustment is not specified in advance but is the outcome of variations in the economic indicator selected as the standard. The adjustment follows changes in the cost of living or changes in the general level of earnings and wages, or a change in the minimum wage, or a combination of factors. The legislation specifies which cost of living index is to be used or which method must be applied to assess variations in the general level of wages or earnings. Some countries, in which adjustment is made on the basis of the cost of living, have promulgated, on certain occasions, special legislation to reduce the gap between the movement in the consumer price index and the wage index so as to allow the elderly to benefit from the general rise in incomes. In at least one country, adjustment is made on the basis of changes in both wages *and* prices. Some countries have special adjustment techniques.

For example, in Sweden, which has both a universal and an earnings-related pension, the calculation of the two pensions is related to a base amount which is the subject of periodic revision as a result of movements in prices. Consequently, any change in the base amount automatically brings about an adjustment of the pension. Moreover, although in the majority of countries the adjustment co-efficient is applied identically no matter what the amount of pension, in certain systems, in contrast, there is only partial adjustment for pensions above a certain level.

The adjustment is made periodically at a set date or on variable dates as soon as the change in the index has reached a specified level (usually 2 to 8 per cent). The interval varies considerably from one country to another. Most often it is annual but it may also be less frequent e.g. every two or three years. In many countries the interval may be much shorter, for example every six months or every three months. In countries with a high rate of inflation the interval has to be short. However, in cases of rapid inflation, even an interval of three months will not prevent a large gap building up between changes in the economic environment and the adjustment of pensions. In many countries which stipulate a regular interval, the adjustment takes place on the prescribed date only if the rise in the price index has reached at least a certain percentage. In one country, which has adopted a two-yearly interval, the indexation will occur earlier should the index increase by more than 8 per cent during the year.

As already indicated, in schemes which link pensions to wages, the adjustment of pensions to variations in economic conditions involves adjustment not only of the pensions currently being paid but also of new pensions, especially where wages taken into consideration relate to relatively distant periods of time. In general, the mechanisms of automatic adjustment provide for the revaluation of reference earnings (average earnings over a certain number of years) on which the pension amount is calculated. The revaluation coefficients are usually the same as the pension adjustment coefficients for pensions currently in payment. Different techniques may be used for these index increases. For example, in one country the key factor is the average annual wage calculated each year for all the insured persons. Each year, a calculation is made of the ratio between the insured person's wages and the annual average wage. The average of this ratio, calculated on all years of insurance, is then used to determine the reference wage. In many African countries, use is made of the "points" method by means of which the insured person acquires, each year, a number of points calculated on the basis of contributions paid (i.e., the level of earnings). The pension equals the number of contribution points acquired by the insured person at the time the benefit is claimed, multiplied by the value of the point for the benefit.

Adjustment in principle

With this method, the law restricts itself to establishing the principle of adjustment without specifying the rules and procedures. This method is in use in many countries, especially in the developing world. It is the responsibility of the competent authority, taking into account the financial situation of the scheme, to decide on the advisability, time and amount of the pension adjustment when it is felt necessary. In many countries, however, the law prescribes the minimum interval at which the adjustment of benefits should, in principle, occur. This varies between one and five years.

Depending on the system, the legislation may provide that the benefit adjustment is to be determined relative to changes in the cost of living, wage levels, minimum wages or a combination of factors. In the majority of these cases, the adjustment cannot take place unless the change recorded is "appreciable" or "significant." Some countries, particularly in Africa, draw on the relevant provisions of ILO instruments. In this way, ILO Convention No. 102 (Article 66) states that "the rates of current periodical payments in respect of old-age, ... shall be reviewed following substantial changes in the general level of earnings where these result from substantial changes in the cost of living." According to the legislation pension rates may be changed, taking into account financial provisions, on the grounds of changes in the general level of wages resulting from a change in the cost of living and depending on the increase in the guaranteed occupational minimum wage. In many legislations the adjustment is contingent upon a prior actuarial study concerning the financial situation of the social security system, which must be taken into account in this decision.

Ad hoc adjustments

The need to adjust pensions to changes in the economic situation obviously will also arise in countries in which the legislation does *not* expressly provide for an adjustment of this type. In some of these countries, pension adjustments are undertaken when they become necessary. This applies in particular to countries in which benefits are set at a uniform rate. From time to time, the benefits are re-adjusted by virtue of special measures. For some countries, there is also a certain regularity in these adjustments, for example, each year. The *ad hoc* adjustment method was also used in the centrally planned economy countries prior to liberalization.

In the same way as for flat-rate pensions, the minimum earnings-related pensions are also increased ad hoc in those countries which have adopted automatic adjustment of pensions.

Application of the different adjustment systems

In the years that preceded the economic crisis which affected many developing countries in the 1980's, the various adjustment methods all made it possible to suitably adapt pensions to changes in economic conditions. A study carried out by the ILO in 1977, which dealt with the movement in the level of benefits in 12 market-economy countries, showed that pensions had, in fact, more than maintained their purchasing power over the period 1963-1975 – regardless of the adjustment method used.

Nevertheless it is widely held that automatic adjustment systems offer considerable advantages from the point of view of the pensioners. This is because pensioners can be certain that their pensions will always be adjusted to variations in economic conditions, so that their real value is at least maintained. Any pension adjustment must necessarily lead to an increase in expenditure; however, it is easier to deal with if the rate of adjustment is not too high and this means that adjustment should be made at not too widely spaced intervals. The prolonged postponement of revisions, which may occur in *ad hoc* adjustment systems, enlarges the gap between the existing pension level and the revised pension level so that the financing of the necessary adjustments may raise severe problems. Consequently, the adjustment may become very inadequate. For example, if the adjustments are carried out infrequently and do not bear a close relationship to the rate of inflation, which has been the case in some countries, pensions will progressively lose a major part of their real value.

In addition, the majority of countries which have aimed at guaranteeing that pensioners participate in economic prosperity have introduced more or less automatic indexation formulae. Certain developing countries have introduced a relatively effective mixed system. Without adopting the principle of automatic indexation, they have nevertheless selected a formula which allows systematic adjustment of the minimum pension depending on the movement in the guaranteed inter-professional minimum wage. This formula is attractive because, in certain of the schemes in question, minimum pensions will amount to 60 to 90 per cent of all pensions paid, depending on the country.

In general, the progress achieved towards better adjustment has nevertheless been held back in a growing number of countries as a result of economic crises and financial difficulties with which pension schemes have been confronted.

C. *Slowing down pension adjustment*

Beginning at the end of the 1970's, an increasing number of countries, while not questioning the principle of adjustment, have modified their systems for containing pension expenditure. Different approaches, implemented separately or in combination, have been used to slow down the increases in expenditure.

One technique frequently employed has been to change the indexes that had previously been used or to adopt a different index. In this way, many countries changed the index which was used as a basis for increasing pensions whilst excluding certain expenditure items from their calculations. For example, in one country only the price rises attributable to internal factors were taken into account in the cost-of-living index. Another country temporarily changed its price indexing system by excluding from the calculation base a number of items such as indirect taxes, import duties and energy prices. In yet another country, the wage index took into account the unemployment rate so that a 1 per cent unemployment rate reduced the index by around 0.5 points.

A large number of countries have adopted a variety of index systems. What has been done, for example, is to replace the wage index by the price index or by an average index of wages and prices. One country has now adopted whichever is the lower of the wage or price index and another country has abandoned a system which took into account the rise in the prices or wages index, whichever was the larger, and has now adopted indexation on prices. Yet another country has suppressed the special reference to the rise in the living standards of employed workers. Several countries have replaced gross wage indexation by net wage indexation.

Another approach used by some countries has been to delay the uprating of pensions, for example by putting back in time the effects of adjustment by suspending indexation for a certain period. Others have put back the dates of benefit adjustments.

Yet another approach is that of placing a ceiling on pension uprating. This has been used in various countries. The technique used in some high-inflation countries, at the suggestion of international financial institutions, has been to replace uprating in proportion to the pension amount (for example 50 per cent) by a flat-rate increase. This technique has certainly made it possible to reduce the growth in pension expenditure in nominal value. However, when repeated several times over, it has resulted in the pension amount being almost the same for everybody, which is a regrettable consequence in a social insurance scheme in which pensions are, in principle, earnings-related.

Finally, certain countries have changed the period taken into consideration for adjustment. For example, one country now links the growth in benefits to the predicted movement in the current year's index and no longer to past variations in the preceding year. In other countries, indexation is no longer made on the past movement in prices but on their forecast movement.

These measures are a one-off response to financial difficulties. However, fundamentally questioning the adjustment measures also introduces significant disadvantages. First, some of these measures produce only short-term effects. For example, in earnings-related pension schemes (in which the benefits follow movements in wages) postponing or suspending indexation has only transitory effects. However, the cumulative effect of these measures, over time, will mean a progressive degradation in the living standard of the elderly and in inequalities between them, depending on the date on which their pension was awarded. Moreover, restricted indexation, in a disguised form, threatens to undermine the contractual basis of pension schemes and, over the longer term, bring about a loss of confidence.

PENSION SCHEMES

MODULE 3:
INVALIDITY BENEFITS

International Labour Office - Geneva

MODULE CONTENTS

53

MODULE 3

INVALIDITY BENEFITS

UNIT 1: Definition and assessment of invalidity

A. Linkage between sickness, invalidity and old-age

Invalidity benefits, in the same way as old-age benefits, may be paid either by non-contributory schemes covering all residents, or by social insurance schemes that apply to only insured workers or, yet again, by provident funds.

Fig. 7:
"linkages between sickness, invalidity and old age ..."

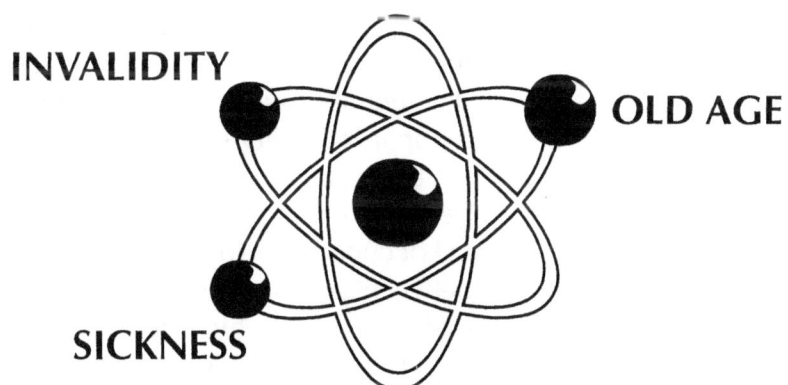

INVALIDITY

OLD AGE

SICKNESS

Depending on the national legislation, invalidity may be considered as premature old-age (with invalidity benefits consequently being grouped together with old-age benefits) or as a prolonged or incurable disease (with benefits then being linked with cash sickness benefits).

The concept of premature old-age was behind the first legislation on this subject, the German Act of 1889, in which old-age was viewed as a type of invalidity. It is also the approach which the ILO international labour standards tend to have adopted in that they put forward parallel rules for invalidity, old-age and survivors' benefits. Grouping together invalidity with old-age contingencies is an approach adopted by many countries.

Origin of invalidity

National legislations usually make a distinction depending on the origin of the invalidity. Invalidity schemes, in most cases, apply only to invalidity resulting from non-occupational diseases/accidents or conditions caused by premature physical deterioration. Congenital invalidity, invalidity suffered by a war veteran and invalidity caused by an employment accident or occupational disease are usually the subject of separate legislation.

In general, disabled persons whose invalidity is due to an occupational or war injury obtain more generous compensation. In the case of invalidity of occupational origin, this applies whether they are covered by a branch with particular responsibility for the compensation of employment accidents and occupational diseases, or are subject to special regulations within the general invalidity benefit system. The situation is quite different for congenital invalidity or early invalidity in children or adolescents. Only a few countries, in which pensions are paid on condition of residence, provide these persons with the same level of benefits as for other beneficiaries. Many of those countries have provided special lower allowances than those in social insurance. However, in the majority of countries, these types of disabilities are covered by social assistance.

Some countries have introduced a unified invalidity system treating all disabled according to similar principles. In spite of these examples, the majority of countries continue to maintain differential protection. This is sometimes criticized because it is felt that invalidity should be compensated in the same way no matter what the cause of the loss of working capacity, and because it is unjust to give preference to persons with invalidity of occupational origin. In particular, the demarcation line between accidents and diseases of proven occupational origin and those in which this is not the case is tenuous. This differentiation gives rise to legal disputes which are of considerable cost to the individual and to society, especially when occupational accident and disease compensation is administered by private insurance companies. It is also pointed out that the work environment is not totally distinct from the environment in which people spend the remainder of their lives.

Attitudes toward invalidity

The differences which have been introduced are not solely of historical origin; they are also based on attitudes toward invalidity. The fact is that the victims of occupational accidents (or disabled war veterans) are considered by the wider population as being victims of action carried out for the benefit of the community and this is the reason for more generous compensation, even though such preferential treatment may not be socially justifiable. Moreover, certain occupational activities involve a special degree of risk.

The problem is therefore a very difficult one. In general, public opinion supports the view that the victims of employment injuries and war wounded *should* benefit from particularly favourable provisions. In addition, unification would seem acceptable only if the unified system is aligned with the most advantageous existing approaches, which would imply a relatively high cost. This perhaps explains why there has been little progress towards the adoption of a unified system of invalidity benefits in most countries.

B. Definition of invalidity

From the social security point of view, a distinction can be made between three different concepts of invalidity: physical invalidity, occupational invalidity and general invalidity.

Physical invalidity

Physical invalidity means a reduction of physical or mental capabilities as the result of the loss of, or impairment to, an organ or function. Reduction of ability is assessed by comparison with the condition of a person in good health. The effect on physical integrity is taken into consideration no matter what the impact on working or earning capacity.

Since the purpose of social security is to protect the individual, in the event of the loss of or marked reduction in earnings from employment, the concept of physical invalidity is rarely retained in national invalidity pension systems. When it is, it is in a subsidiary manner – in cases in which the lesion is not scheduled in the law – or in a complementary manner. (It is, in contrast, retained in legislation on the war wounded and in several occupational risk compensation legislations).

Occupational invalidity

In the case of occupational invalidity, the individual's invalidity is assessed in relation to the loss of earning capacity resulting from being unfit to resume the work previously done. Schemes which apply occupational invalidity, in the strict definition of the term, are certain special schemes and, in particular, schemes for miners. For example, a miner is considered to be suffering from occupational invalidity if he is unable to perform his previous occupation, or any similar occupation remunerated in the same way and normally performed by people with similar training and the same occupational abilities.

Occupational invalidity may also be given a much wider definition. The degree of invalidity is assessed on the basis of all occupations comparable or similar to that of the applicant and reclassification opportunities may be sought within a framework much larger than that of the enterprise.

General invalidity

The general degree of invalidity is assessed in relation to residual work capacity and the level of income that a person may still derive from work compatible with his or her health status. The residual work capacity is assessed in relation to *any* type of work and not just in relation to a single occupation – as is the case of occupational invalidity.

Often, the legislation does not adhere strictly to one concept of invalidity to the exclusion of others. A scheme may incorporate both the general and occupational concept of invalidity, both of which may be applied at the same time.

Degree of invalidity

Whichever concept is used for defining invalidity, benefit entitlement is always subject to the fact that the severity of the incapacity must always exceed a certain level. This "threshold" varies appreciably from one country to another. Although many legislations specify the degree in terms of a percentage, others prefer not to make such a specification. Where it is specified, it is often around 66 per cent or two-thirds.

In several countries there are two or more degrees of invalidity, a differentiation that was introduced after the Second World War. A distinction is thus made between "total (or near total) invalidity" and "partial invalidity, resulting in a significant reduction in work capacity but with retention of the ability to engage in gainful employment up to a certain degree".

In many countries, account is also taken of the fact that the disabled person is required to call on the assistance of a third party in order to carry out normal living functions. In such cases, the rate of pension is increased or an additional benefit, sometimes called a constant attendance allowance, is paid.

C. Invalidity assessment and revision

The establishment of effective methods of assessing invalidity is the foundation of invalidity benefit administration. Invalidity, as defined in the law, has to be assessed on the basis of prescribed criteria, by an authority which is competent in relation to each benefit request, although the initial assessment can be re-examined at a subsequent date.

Rules for applicable criteria

National legislations lay down the criteria which must be applied in assessing invalidity and determining its severity. Some of these criteria may vary from country to country or one country may attribute more or less importance to one or another criterion.

One general, basic criterion is that physical or mental disability must reduce the applicant's work capacity. The health status found at the time of assessment must be of a relatively stable nature. In some countries, the possible effect of continuing to work on the health status of the applicant is taken into account. The person may be judged to be totally disabled if it appears that returning to regular work would be sufficient to constitute a serious threat to his or her health.

In virtually all cases, non-medical factors are also taken into account. For example, occupational factors and, in several countries, other social factors will often be considered.

The occupational factors include age, education and occupational experience for these factors indicate the range of work that the applicant would normally be able to undertake. The more restricted the range, the more the applicant's physical or mental limitations will be such as to prevent engaging in gainful employment.

Age is an important factor to the extent that the same disabilities and health problems usually have more severe consequences for the elderly than for younger persons. Age is a factor to be considered when assessing vocational rehabilitation potential. Many countries take age into consideration, as well as the applicant's level of education and work experience.

There are also many countries which look at other social factors, such as the applicant's family environment, opportunities for vocational training or the possibility of moving to another part of the country. As far as this latter criterion is concerned, the possibility of a disabled worker actually engaging in gainful employment may depend, to a large extent, on the place where (s)he lives or the place where (s)he would be employed. In a wider context, certain countries also take into consideration the conditions of the labour market. However, in view of the current employment situation and the way in which the function of invalidity benefits has changed in some countries (where it has tended to become virtually a form of unemployment benefit) use of such a criterion tends to become more difficult.

In order to establish the claimant's health and occupational status and situation, in relation to other criteria laid down in national legislation, it is necessary to assemble the evidence for processing the claim. In general, the claimant and the invalidity benefit administration authority share the responsibility of establishing and assembling the necessary information.

Competent authorities for invalidity assessment

The person or body responsible for assessing invalidity varies considerably from country to country. The choice of this person or body is important for it will have a significant effect on the success of the scheme.

Since the criteria for determining invalidity very often include medical, occupational and sometimes other factors, it seems necessary, in principle, to involve specialists from various disciplines (physicians, professionals, members of the legal profession, etc.).

In practice, the situation varies considerably from country to country.

If medical criteria are dominant (or exclusive), a physician, a medical institution or an authorized medical commission will usually have competence. If this is not the case, physicians and non-medical personnel (occupational experts, social workers, members of the legal profession) may act jointly in the matter. The final decision may be taken by the specialists responsible for invalidity assessment or by a neutral administrator (from a social security scheme or administrative tribunal) who will use, but not necessarily exclusively, the prior reports drawn up by the specialists. Whichever formula is adopted it should be noted that, other than for those cases where there is no doubt, invalidity assessment raises sensitive problems since its assessment relies on discretionary judgement.

Table 2 provides a comparison of the definition of invalidity used in the benefit schemes of various countries.

Table 2: Invalidity benefits in selected countries.

Country	Definition of invalidity
Algeria	Loss of all working capacity (if 50% loss, partial pension).
Argentina	Reduction in earning capacity by 66% (total disability).
Australia	Minimum 20% level of impairment and inability to work full-time at full wages for the forseeable future.
Belgium	Loss of 2/3 earning capacity in usual occupation.
Brazil	Permanent incapacity for work.
China	Total incapacity for work.
Estonia	Full or partial or long-term disability for work.
Finland	Permanent incapacity for suitable work. (Also: earnings-related pension for 3/5 loss of work capacity of 2/5 loss for a partial pension).
Hungary	Total disability (incapacity for any paid work). Partial disability (67% loss of working capacity).
Indonesia*	Total incapacity for work and under age 55.
Iraq	Permanent or long-continued loss of 35% of working capacity.
Ireland	Permanent incapacity for work (payable after 1 years' ordinary sickness benefit.
Libya	80% loss of earning capacity in last job or other suitable work.
Mauritius	60% disability for at least 12 months.
Phillipines	Permanent and total disablement.
Uganda*	Total incapacity for any work or permanent partial incapacity causing inability to earn a reasonable livelihood.
Zambia*	Permanent incapacity for any work due to physical or mental disability.

* Provident fund

Source: U.S. Social Security Administration, *Social security programs throughout the world — 1995,* Washington, D.C., 1995.

Appeals

In general, claimants and the social security institution both have the right to appeal against decisions on whether claims for invalidity benefits are receivable. There are countries where opportunities for prior administrative appeal need to be exhausted before the matter can be brought before a court. In others, appeals are submitted directly to the courts or, where necessary, to specialized jurisdictions. Appeals may be purely legal or aim to establish additional proof, and in particular medical proof.

Review of the initial assessment

Although the concept of invalidity usually implies that the person's condition has more or less stabilized, legislations usually contain provisions for the review of an initial assessment.

The principle of review is normally accepted, except where the disease definitely seems incurable and rehabilitation appears impossible. The pension is not awarded for life. Invalidity beneficiaries are usually required to report any change in their status which might influence their invalidity pension entitlement. Alternatively, a review will often be provided for on a routine basis and it may take place at regular intervals (for example, once per year). In this way, social security institutions are compelled to take certain control measures so as to determine whether a review is necessary.

In some countries, the legislation usually specifies the party which has the right to request review, the reasons and the intervals between reviews. If, for example, a country introduces major changes in the circumstances surrounding the award of invalidity pensions, cases may be reviewed at any time.

Often it is the person or agency responsible for the assessment of invalidity who decides how and when a review should take place. This will take into account the individual features and, in particular, the type and severity of the injury or disability and its probable evolution.

In addition, some legislations specifically provide for a temporary pension, which is granted for a period laid down in advance.

UNIT 2: Qualifying conditions and calculation of benefits

A. *Conditions for awarding pensions*

Qualifying period

Invalidity pension entitlement is subject to completion of a specified qualifying period. This is a minimum duration of insurance, employment or residence, as evidence of a sufficiently lengthy period of coverage in the scheme. The purpose is to prevent abuse and to avoid situations of adverse selection.

Residence conditions are usually required by those schemes in which the award of a benefit does not depend on the direct financial participation of the protected person (or his or her employer) or on a period of employment. The qualifying period required is laid down in different ways depending on the legislation in question. In those national pension systems which are applicable to all residents, the "length of residence conditions" are often the same as those for old-age pensions. However, in other schemes, the residence conditions may be significantly lower.

Fig. 8:
"Qualifying conditions for benefits"

In insurance schemes, the qualifying period is the minimum period of time for which the insured person must have been insured or employed (including, where appropriate, periods assimilated to periods of contribution or employment). In general, the qualifying period required for an invalidity pension is significantly lower than that prescribed for an old-age pension. The required qualifying period may be specified in relation to the total minimum period required. Frequently this is based on a minimum period of insurance during a specified period of time immediately preceding the determination of invalidity: for example, 60 months of insurance, 12 of which must have been accomplished during the past three years, or 60 months of insurance over the past 10 years.

In certain countries the required qualifying period varies, depending on the age of the insured person: the period is longer, once a certain age has been reached, e.g. age 25 or 30. In the United States, the qualifying period varies in proportion to age: one of the conditions is that the insured person must have one calendar quarter of insurance for each year since age 21 until the year of disability (as well as 20 calendar quarters of insurance in the 10 year period prior to onset).

In the majority of schemes, the qualifying period does not exceed five years of insurance. The length of the stipulated qualifying period is much shorter in countries in which invalidity insurance is considered to be a prolongation of sickness benefit (for temporary incapacity): for example, 120 days of work over the past six months.

Other conditions for awarding a pension

In certain countries, for example many African countries, invalidity pensions are in fact seen as early retirement pensions. A minimum age condition is therefore provided. For example, an insured person has to be at least 50 years of age in order to claim an invalidity pension.

In some schemes which are applicable to all residents, a means test is prescribed. The majority of schemes applicable to all residents also include a nationality condition.

B. Calculating benefits

Depending on the principle that has been adopted (guaranteeing a minimum level of income or maintenance of a standard of living related to that during the period of employment) the invalidity pension amount, may be either at a uniform rate, or related to wages or earnings in the same way as the old-age pension amount.

Uniform-rate pensions

For flat-rate invalidity pensions, the benefit is either the same as for old-age pensions or at least closely linked to it. Where means testing has been stipulated for old-age pensions, the same usually applies to invalidity pensions, except perhaps in the case of blind persons.

In many countries in which the invalidity pension amount varies depending on the degree of incapacity, disabled persons classified at the highest degree of incapacity are entitled to a pension amount equal to that for an old-age pension; the pensions payable to the disabled classified in the other groups are at lower levels.

In Denmark, where the legislation distinguishes between three invalidity groups, the pension is made up of three components: a base amount subject to means testing; a supplement for invalidity; a supplement for incapacity for gainful employment. The base amount is equal to the amount of an old-age pension for maximum invalidity and it is lower for minimum invalidity.

In other countries, the invalidity pension amount is the same as for an old-age pension, but it is supplemented if the invalidity occurs before the insured person has reached a certain age.

Earnings-related pensions

As a general rule, all countries which have earnings related old-age pensions also have earnings related invalidity pensions. In many of these countries, the invalidity pension amount is calculated using a formula similar to that for old-age pensions. The amount is therefore determined on the basis of the reference wage and also the duration of insurance.

Since the link with the duration of insurance, contribution or employment is likely to result in very small pension amounts, if the disability occurs when the insured person has been insured for only a short period, a correction is usually introduced. In some countries, a special minimum figure is provided for and this is either equal to a percentage of earnings or is a prescribed amount.

In many other countries, the period of insurance, contribution or employment which has actually been completed by the insured person is increased by a supplementary period, in contrast to the way in which old-age pensions are calculated. The periods from the onset of the disability to the date on which the insured person reaches a prescribed age are counted as (assimilated to) periods of insurance. This prescribed age may be higher than, equal to or lower than the qualifying age for an old-age pension. These added periods ensure that workers who become disabled, before the end of a normal occupational career, receive an invalidity pension which is very close (if not equal) to that of the old-age pension they would have been able to claim. Thus, in some schemes, the benefit is calculated as though the applicant had worked up to the age of 55 years whilst, in others, the period up to the pensionable age is added to the effective periods of insurance. There are also schemes in which a prescribed percentage of the period between the onset of disability and the normal pensionable age is added to periods of insurance.

Finally, it should be noted that the reference wage, used as a basis for calculating pensions, may be defined differently for old-age and invalidity pensions. For example, the invalidity benefit will be calculated on the basis of average earnings during the 12 month period immediately preceding the contingency whereas, for calculation of an old-age pension, the average earnings will be calculated over a much longer period.

Other formulae

The solutions adopted by national legislations for calculating invalidity pensions on the basis of wages or earnings are extremely varied. Usually they involve the duration of insurance only to a limited degree or even take no account of it at all. For example, the invalidity pension may be made up of a fixed sum and a variable amount. In several countries in which invalidity insurance is closely linked to sickness insurance – so that invalidity insurance is seen, to a certain extent, as the prolongation of initial temporary incapacity benefits – the duration of insurance does not enter into account, except of course, as far as the qualifying period is concerned. In one of these countries, for example, the pension is equal to 50 per cent of the reference wage in the case of total invalidity and 30 per cent in the case of partial invalidity. In another country, the pension ranges between 10% and 80% of the reference wage, depending on the degree of invalidity. It should be noted in this context that, where there are several degrees of invalidity, the amount of the partial invalidity benefit is reduced in relation to that of the total invalidity benefit.

In a provident fund system, the invalidity benefit is in the form of a lump-sum payment and is the amount to the insured person's credit supplemented by accrued interest. In some countries, even if the disability is relatively minor, the payment of a lump sum is permitted.

Supplements for the severely disabled

There are also schemes which provide a supplement for those severely disabled who require the constant presence of a third person. In the majority of these countries, this supplement is reserved for the beneficiaries of an invalidity pension. However, in schemes in which an invalidity pension is converted to an old-age pension at the pensionable age, the supplement received by beneficiaries before this age is maintained.

The amount of the supplement is calculated in different ways from country to country. It is obviously independent of a reference wage in all schemes which pay flat-rate invalidity pensions. It may also be a fixed amount in other schemes. In the majority, however, the supplement is expressed as a percentage of the reference wage for the invalidity pension. It may happen that the supplement varies, depending on whether the disabled person requires occasional or regular assistance (during the day or round-the-clock) or depending on his or her family situation.

Cumulating a pension with other earnings or with an old-age pension

Some countries have adopted rules authorizing the cumulation of a pension and the earnings that a disabled person may derive from gainful employment, with a view to encouraging these people to return to work. Usually, a ceiling is placed on earnings so that cumulation is possible. In certain countries, the invalidity pension may still be paid within prescribed limits if the disabled person regains a working capacity greater than the maximum capacity adopted in the definition of invalidity.

In contrast, other national legislations prescribe the suppression of the pension should the person resume gainful activity, with the exception of low-paying activities that are compatible with the beneficiary's health status.

It is also accepted practice that the invalidity pension cannot be received together with the old-age pension. The majority of legislations specify that the disability must occur *before* the prescribed age for an old-age pension and that the invalidity pension is replaced by an old-age pension once pensionable age has been attained. The conversion of an invalidity pension into an old-age pension is often automatic, even if the qualifying period specified for the old-age pension has not been completed, although there may be exceptions to this rule. Although several legislations specify that the old-age pension may not be lower than the invalidity pension which it replaces, in others the old age pension may be lower (or equal or higher) if the rules for determining the pension amount are different for the two contingencies.

C. *Vocational rehabilitation and retraining*

In all countries, the invalidity pension system is designed to make use of rehabilitation and retraining measures for the persons suffering from or at risk of invalidity. These measures aim to re-introduce these persons into society. However, the complex problems related to the rehabilitation and retraining of disabled persons, especially when the labour market is in a difficult situation, should not be underestimated.

Fig. 9:

"... rehabilitation and retraining measures ..."

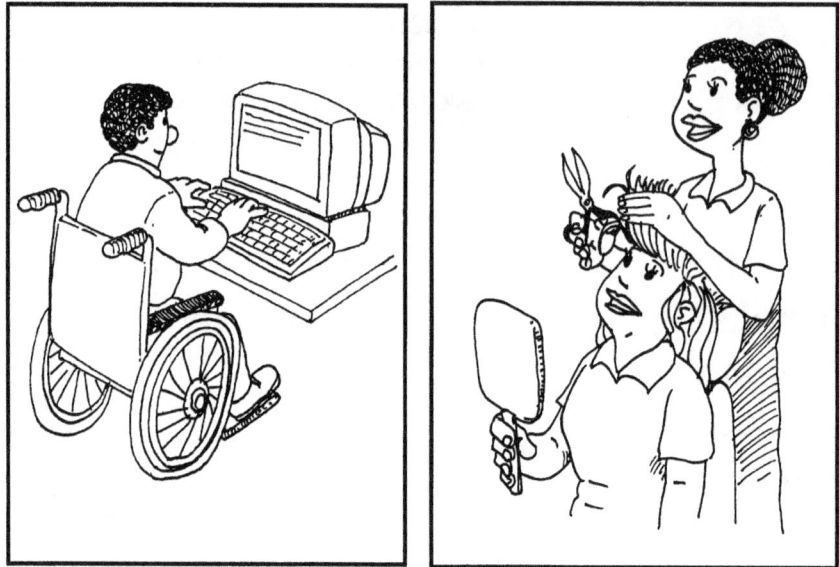

Several legislations stipulate that the agency administering invalidity insurance should set up rehabilitation services or bear the cost of treatment. In other countries, these services are organized and financed in a different way although there is still close co-ordination between them and the invalidity insurance scheme.

In order to facilitate vocational rehabilitation and make it as effective as possible, social security legislations sometimes prescribe measures to encourage the beneficiary to undertake rehabilitation. One such measure is to pay special benefits to insured persons during rehabilitation, for example, subsistence allowances and rehabilitation supplements.

Countries which have ratified the Invalidity, Old-Age and Survivors' Benefits Convention, 1967 (No. 128) are required to "provide rehabilitation services which are designed to prepare a disabled person, wherever possible, for the resumption of his previous activity or, if this is not possible, the most suitable alternative gainful activity, having regard to his aptitudes and capacity" as well as to "take measures to further the placement of disabled persons in suitable employment."

PENSION SCHEMES

MODULE 4:
SURVIVORS' BENEFITS

International Labour Office - Geneva

MODULE CONTENTS

MODULE 4

SURVIVORS' BENEFITS

UNIT 1: Qualifying conditions

A. Dependency and the family

One of the objectives of social security is to provide protection in the event of the death of the family breadwinner, including assistance in adapting to the new circumstances resulting from the loss of support previously provided to the family. The death of the breadwinner gives rise both to exceptional expenses and a permanent loss of income for the family. There are three main categories of benefits on the death of an insured insured person: lump-sum payments to meet the additional costs incurred at the time of the death; pensions or allowances paid to the surviving spouse; and benefits for children or other dependent family members.

Fig. 10:
*"Three main categories ...
lump sum ...
pension ...
dependants".*

Survivors' benefits are characterized by the fact that beneficiaries must have a specific relationship with another person who is usually protected against a risk such as old age or invalidity, in other words, who is related to an insured (or protected) person. Most old-age pension schemes therefore incorporate survivors' benefits. (A separate category of survivor benefits are provided in the event of death due to employment injury). Survivors' pensions are intended to compensate for the loss of economic support previously provided by the deceased person. The extent of the loss depends on the age and earnings of the breadwinner, the age and number of dependants, the amount of the support that was provided for each dependant and the length of time the support would have been expected to continue. The ability of family members to be self-supporting may also be a consideration.

The majority of beneficiaries of survivors' benefit schemes are women and children. However, changes in society and developments in the labour market (notably the growth of women's employment and changes in family life styles such as increases in divorce and cohabitation out of wedlock) have led to a re-examination of existing legislation on survivors' benefits in several countries, in particular as they relate to the concepts of dependence and equality of treatment between men and women. The central problem to be addressed concerns the surviving spouse. The situation of orphans and dependent parents raises less controversy and fewer difficulties.

Fig. 11:
Dependency and the family

B. The surviving spouse

The widow beneficiary

The main beneficiary in survivors' benefits schemes is still the widow. However, the provisions that apply to her differ from one country to another. An appreciable number of schemes, in both industrialized and developing countries, award a survivor's pension to the widow without any special conditions. The widow is therefore presumed to have been supported by the deceased insured husband. Nevertheless, in many of these schemes, widows who do not fulfill certain conditions can only claim a reduced pension.

There are also many legislations which do not recognize a presumption of need on the part of the widow, unless certain conditions about family situation, age and/or health status have been met.

Before examining these questions, mention should be made of those countries which practice polygamy. Where the joint spouse has died, the benefit prescribed for the widow is shared out between the wives. In general, this share-out is definitive, i.e. the pension for each widow will not be recalculated even if one of the wives subsequently dies.

The family situation of the widow

The family situation may have an impact on the award of a benefit, from several points of view. Was the "widow" joined with the deceased person in a legal marriage? If not, does the legislation recognize the *de facto* marriage which marital cohabitation may constitute? How long have the couple been married? Does the widow have to raise the children of this union with the deceased person? Is she expecting his child? Will the widow get married again? Can a previous divorced wife of the deceased person be considered as his widow?

Conditions linked to the marriage

In many countries, the legal marriage between the widow and the deceased person continues to be a necessary condition in order to receive a survivor's benefit. Consequently, these countries do not take into account situations of dependence outside of marriage itself. However, in view of the rapid changes in life styles, the question of recognizing as a couple (for the purposes of social security) the stable relationship of a man and a woman living together is often raised. Many countries already recognize couples who are not legally married, for the purpose of survivors' benefits.

Many legislations make a widow's pension entitlement subject to the condition of a minimal duration of marriage or to the condition that the marriage was contracted before the husband reached a prescribed age (usually the prescribed age for an old-age pension) or a certain length of time before the husband's death. In some countries, this is the *only* condition placed on the widow. The essential purpose of such limitations is to prevent abuses which might result from marriages contracted "in extremis" or contracted at a very late age. As will be seen below, these conditions are not applied when there has been a child from the marriage nor, in certain countries, when the husband's death is the result of a work-related accident.

The length stipulated for the marriage or age at marriage may vary considerably, depending on the legislation. There are schemes in which the pension is payable only if the marriage was contracted at least two years before the deceased began to receive the pension awarded to him, or when the marriage has lasted for at least four years. In one scheme, a minimum marriage duration is stipulated if the husband is drawing a pension on the date of the marriage; there is a variable minimum duration, depending on the age difference between the spouses and this may be as high as ten years for an age difference of over 25 years. In one country in which this condition is not stipulated, a widow without children whose marriage has lasted less than five years is entitled only to a lump sum payment instead of a pension.

As a rule, the widow's pension is discontinued if a widow enters into a new marriage. One country maintains the pension if the widow marries again after the age of 60 years but the amount is reduced. Often, the widow who remarries is entitled to a lump-sum payment amounting to one or more annual payments of her pension.

In the majority of cases, the widow's pension entitlement is terminated definitively in the event of remarriage. However, in some countries, this entitlement may be reinstated in the event of the death of the new husband (or if the marriage results in divorce or is annulled) provided the widow is not entitled to a widow's pension on the grounds of her last marriage.

Widowed mothers

In all legislations which make a widow's pension entitlement subject to a marriage condition, the condition is not applied if a child is born of the marriage (including a posthumous child). A widow who is raising her late husband's children and has them as dependants is usually accepted to be entitled to a pension.

Divorced women

In many countries, a divorced wife may claim a pension on the death of her ex-husband provided that he was required, at the date of his death, to pay her maintenance. Further conditions may be stipulated, for example, a minimum length of marriage or that there are dependent children by the deceased husband. Certain countries establish a close link between the maintenance payment and the pension that a divorced woman may claim.

When a deceased person, after a new marriage, leaves a wife with a survivor's pension entitlement, this pension may be changed, in certain situations, because of the right of a previous spouse also to receive a pension. The amount of the widow's pension is, to some extent, shared between the widow and the ex-spouse in proportion to the length of their respective marriages.

Age conditions

In many schemes, a widow is entitled to the survivor's pension *only* if she has reached a prescribed age at the date of the death of the husband, or after this date. In many of these schemes, the minimum age required to obtain entitlement to the widow's pension is lower than that specified for old-age pensions.

The stipulated age varies considerably according to the legislation. It may be relatively low, for example, 35 years, or it may be closer to the pensionable age, e.g. age 50. In several countries it is the same as the pensionable age. Some legislations stipulate a double age limit and the pension is then paid at a reduced rate in the period between the two age limits. For example, a normal pension might be awarded if the widow is more than 50 years old; if she is under 50 years of age but more than 40, she may claim a reduced pension. Under other legislations, the pension reduction, in the case of women who have not reached the specified age, is scaled depending on their age. Thus the reduction is less for those who have reached an age which is close to the age limit.

In some countries, the beneficiary must have reached the pensionable age for a widow's pension by the date of the death of the husband. In more countries, it is sufficient if she has reached this age after this date. Many, however, specificy a limit: for example, the widow must have reached the stipulated age within the five years following the death of her husband. In this case, a young widow will never receive the widow's pension.

In a general way, setting a minimum age for awarding a pension is based on the idea that a young widow, who is fit for work and who has no dependent family, should be in a position to enter gainful employment.

Nevertheless, no matter what the widow's age it is certain that, during an initial period, widowhood does result in a profound change in her situation. The income earned by the late husband disappears but family expenditure is not reduced to the same degree. Housing needs will remain the same, at least for a time, and general household expenditure often continues without reduction. A period of time is therefore essential to adapt the surviving spouse's living conditions to her new situation.

Consequently, many legislations provide for temporary assistance during the initial period of widowhood. This assistance may be a lump-sum payment, either calculated on a flat-rate basis, or in relation to the deceased person's last earnings. The assistance is more effective if it takes the form of temporary periodic benefits in favour of those widows who have no pension entitlement. In this way, it enables the survivor to make the necessary adjustments to her life style, perhaps to obtain training and to look for gainful employment. A number of countries award these widows a temporary pension for a variable period of time, usually one year or less. One country pays a pension to all widows which is supplemented, during the first three months of widowhood, so as to reach the amounts of the old-age pension to which the deceased spouse had been (or would have been) entitled. In another country, the widow may receive assistance in obtaining vocational training so as to be more readily able to find gainful employment.

Disabled widows

A number of legislations provide for the award of a widow's pension to the widow who has not fulfilled the age conditions or the conditions relating to child maintenance, if she is disabled. It should be pointed out that invalid widows are not considered as a distinct category in countries in which invalidity insurance covers all residents. In these countries the invalid widow, in the same way as any other protected person, is entitled to a pension on a personal basis and not as a widow.

The widow's invalidity is usually assessed on the basis of her residual work capacity, which may allow her to engage in gainful employment, i.e., according to the same principle as in invalidity insurance. However, there is never any classification of invalids, on the basis of their degree of work incapacity, that is encountered in invalidity insurance schemes. The definition of disabilty may also be different from that of invalidity insurance, in that there is a requirement to meet stricter criteria. For example in one country, in which an invalidity benefit is awarded if the rate of incapacity is at least two-thirds, the invalid widow will receive a pension only if she is entirely incapable of carrying out any gainful employment. In another country, in which an invalidity pension is awarded starting with an incapacity of 25 per cent, the widow's disability must be at least 50 per cent.

Usually, the disability must exist at the date of the spouse's death but a certain number of schemes recognize the pension entitlement, even if invalidity occurs at a later date.

In the same way as for invalidity pensions, widows' pensions awarded under the heading of invalidity are no longer paid (except where the widow has reached the age required to be entitled to a widow's pension without other conditions) should the person recover to such a degree that she no longer meets the degree of incapacity required for the pension.

Review of a widow's pension

Social security legislations almost always recognize the entitlement of widows to a pension. However, as has been seen, the conditions required for awarding such benefits vary considerably from one country to another. It might be argued that a high level of female labour force participation would justify a system in which widows' pensions were limited to categories who are unable to meet their own needs. For example in Denmark, the widow's pension (and the disability pension) were eliminated in 1984 and replaced by a universal "early pension" for *all* residents who have reduced working capacity and whose income is below certain limits. It might also be assumed that the recognition of pension entitlement for all widows would be more the situation in countries in which the employment of women is low; in reality there is little evidence of such a correlation.

In most countries, the traditional view, under which most social security schemes were devised and developed, still prevails: the assumption is that the woman is dependent in the family. Wives were supposed to live from the work done by their husbands, the fathers of their children. Either the wife devoted herself entirely to her home or she was presumed to derive only supplementary income, "pin money," from any gainful employment. If the husband died, the widow, who had not had any gainful employment or who had earned only modest income from her work, either had no individual entitlement to a pension or her entitlement was lower than that which would have allowed her to maintain her previous standard of living. This was the justification for setting up widows' pension schemes calculated on the basis of the old-age pension to which the husband would have been entitled.

Furthermore, this is the view that was reflected in ILO international labour standards, which refer to survivors' benefits for the widow or the child of the breadwinner. In the case of the widow, Convention No. 102 allows "the right to benefit" to be conditional on the widow being incapable of self-support; whereas Convention No. 128 provides that the benefit may be conditional on the attainment of a prescribed age, except in cases of disability and when the widow is caring for a dependent child of the deceased.

However, the distribution of roles in the family is changing. The concept of the woman's economic dependence is less and less in line with the actual situation (it may sometimes be that it is the woman who earns the main income) and it is not in conformity with modern concepts of relations between women and men. Current changes in thinking are influenced by increasing acceptance of the principle of equality of treatment, by the prohibition of any discrimination between men and women and by the rejection of the assumption of dependence, in the partnership, of the woman on the man.

In view of these principles and the new realities, there is a tendency to radically question widows' pensions and to propose different formulae to enable the surviving spouse to maintain a standard of living similar to that which she enjoyed whilst her husband was still alive, i.e., to compensate for the loss of the husband's occupational income.

As already mentioned, temporary assistance for the widow during the initial period of widowhood, in the form of a benefit of limited duration, could be provided, so as to allow the widow to undertake training or retraining in order to find gainful employment.

At the end of that initial period, the surviving spouse – with the exception of those who had reached a certain age – would find herself in the same situation as any other single person and able to work and earn her living in the same way as any other single woman.

Furthermore, a solution could also be found for the problem caused by the inadequacy of the pension which the widow might receive at her retirement age, resulting from her reduced period of insurance. To this end, it would be necessary to extend the woman's individual rights in such a way that they take into account not only her periods of gainful employment, but also the time she devoted to raising any children she may have had, as well as half of the joint pension entitlement acquired by the husband and the wife during the marriage. A number of schemes allow periods of child rearing as assimilated periods of insurance. Both Canada and Germany have adopted the practice of "credit splitting," i.e., sharing the pension entitlements equally between the spouses for the period of the marriage (in the case of Germany only at divorce). The aim is to replace the concept of "derived rights", in pension entitlement, by the individual rights that are acquired by each spouse.

If a woman who has no gainful employment loses her husband at an age which, although lower than the normal qualifying age for an old-age pension, is still too old for her to realistically hope to start or return to gainful employment, an early old-age pension could be provided.

The need for widows' pensions would then seem much less obvious. Those who are promoting the new formulae, described above, consider that they would provide increased security for the surviving spouse and that they would be better adapted to the needs of these spouses than is the current system of widows' pensions. Reforms of this type are only slowly being adopted and in any case can only be introduced progressively, in order to protect the rights of women whose expectations were based on traditional concepts.

C. Widowers' pensions

Not all survivors' benefit schemes recognize the right of a widower to a pension. In those that do, the majority make a pension award subject to conditions which are more restrictive than those imposed in the case of widows' pensions. This entitlement is accepted only if the widower is disabled. Some legislations also stipulate an age condition: the widower must have reached the qualifying age for an old-age pension.

In addition, the majority of legislations make entitlement to a widowers' pension subject to the condition that the person in question was dependent on his wife at the time of her death. In a country which stipulates no age or invalidity condition for the award of a widower's pension, it is specified that the sole condition is that the wife took a predominant part in maintaining the family. In assessing this condition, account is taken not only of the occupational income of the wife but also of the estimated value of her work in the family home.

In many countries, in particular those in which the employment of married women is widespread, it is pointed out that the difference in treatment between widows and widowers is a negation of the principle of equality of treatment between women and men. The denial of widowers' benefits should be seen not only in terms of direct discrimination against men, it is also discrimination against the insured woman who has paid contributions while employed for the protection of her survivors in the event of her death. There is increasing agreement on the principle that pensions should be equally accessible to either surviving spouse. However, as a practical matter, it is not easy to offer a solution to this problem, since there could be considerable costs to the scheme. Equality of treatment, therefore, in some cases has been accompanied by more restrictive eligibility conditions on widows, which are then applied equally to widowers.

D. Orphans' pensions

In the event of the death of the family breadwinner, the children are entitled to periodic benefits. In some countries these benefits can be accumulated with family allowances.

The categories of children who are entitled to benefits varies quite significantly from one country to another. In countries which have a family allowance scheme, this scheme will, as a general rule, have a definition of "the child" for the purposes of benefits and this is then taken over into the survivors' benefits scheme. All schemes provide benefits to legitimate and legitimized children and to natural children. In many countries, adopted children are also recognized as being entitled.

Many schemes lay down the normal age limit, for the payment of survivors' benefits to children, at between 14 and 18 years. Some countries make a distinction in this context between girls and boys (an older age for girls). In the majority of schemes, pension entitlement is extended for several years beyond the normal age limit if the child is continuing vocational training or full-time studies. This higher age may vary between 18 and 27 years. The majority of schemes do not stipulate any age limit for disabled children.

Generally, the pensions for children who are orphaned of both a father and a mother are higher than those for children who lose only one parent. Certain countries pay supplemented family allowances instead of orphans' pensions. It is considered that both formulae are valid in ensuring maintenance of orphans, provided the allowances or pensions are of an adequate amount.

E. Other beneficiaries

A number of schemes also provide benefits to survivors other than the spouse and the children who were dependent on the deceased insured person. The way in which the categories of these survivors – and the conditions required for entitlement to the pension – are determined differ significantly from one scheme to another.

Most frequently, the survivors with pension entitlement are the parents of the deceased person: the mother and the father, and in some schemes, the grandparents. Ascendants usually have to be disabled or elderly to receive a survivors' pension. The minimum age is usually the normal qualifying age for an old-age pension. In many countries, the parents may claim a pension if they do not work and if they take care of the children of the deceased insured person.

In some national legislations, other survivors who may have entitlement are the grandchildren, minor brothers and sisters, non-married sisters or parents-in-law, provided these persons were dependent on the deceased person.

In a very few countries, a pension similar to the widow's pension may be awarded to a person who, in the deceased person's home, undertook the care of the household normally done by the wife.

Usually, the definition of survivors protected by the national scheme reflects the traditional situation, regarding the family, in each country.

In the majority of schemes, however, entitled persons other than the spouse and the children can receive a pension *only* in the second degree, i.e., provided there are no survivors in the priority group.

Table 3 summarises the qualifying conditions for various categories of survivors in selected countries.

Table 1: Survivors' benefits in selected countries

Country	Qualifying survivors
Armenia	Surviving children (whether or not dependants of the insured); non-working dependants (including spouse; either parent-if disabled or not yet of pension age; grandparents, if no other support available).
Austria	Widow/widower; orphans under 18 (27 if a student and no limity if disabled).
Bahrain	Widow; orphans under 22 (26 if a student in higher education); dependent parents, brothers and sisters. Where there is more than one beneficiary, the pension is shared on a percentage basis and the total payable will not exceed 100% of the pension entitlement.
Belarus	Surviving dependent spouse; parents of insured (if of pension age, disabled or caring for a child under 8 and do not work); grandparents (if no one legally responsible for their livelihood); children, siblings and grandchildren under age 18 (23 if a student) or older if disabled before age 18.
Colombia	Spouse or permanent companion; children (less than 18; students between 18 and 25; if disabled-any age) economically dependent on the deceased; dependent parents and dependent siblings.
Dominica	Widow/widower at age 50; if married for less than three years widow/er receives pension for only one year; orphans under 16 (18 if full-time student).
France	Widow at age 55 (50 if widow has a child), divorced or deserted wife, or widower; (at any age if disabled). Pension proportionally divided if more than 1 qualified surviving spouse.
Ghana	Nominated dependants.
Israel	Surviving spouse if age 50 or over, or caring for child (income tested for widowers); reduced pension for widow aged 40-49 with one child; if under 40 and no child, lump sum payment made; orphans.
Jordan	Widow; son under age 18 (no age limit if disabled); unmarried/divorced/dependent daughters; dependent parents; brothers, sisters; widower.
Korea, Republic of	Spouse or child (under age 18 or second degree of disability at any age); parent of insured person (including parent of spouse) or of a pensioner.
Malaysia	Widow; each orphan under 21 (up to first university degree if in school).
Mali	Widow, widower, children under age 14 (age 21 if student or disabled).
Nepal*	Nominee or, if none, heirs of the insured.
New Zealand	Widow; orphans.
Panama	Widow age 55, disabled or caring for child (until child ceases to receive orphan's benefit); other widows for 5 years only; orphans under 14 (18 if student; without limit if disabled); dependant disabled widower; other dependents (in absence of the above): mother or aged/disabled father; eligible brothers and sisters.
Portugal	Widow - limited to 5 years unless over age 35, disabled, or caring for child. Equally paid to (widow or) widower. Orphans; parents or grandparents.

Country	Qualifying survivors
Russian Federation	Each dependent (at least 30% of base wage).
Sudan	Widow (if more than one, divided equally) or dependent widower; children under age 18 (age 26 if student, no limit if disabled or unmarried daughter); parents; dependent brothers and sisters if no one of higher priority.
Togo	Widow age 40 or disabled, widower (if disabled and dependent) children under age 16 (age 18 if apprentice, age 21 if student or disabled).

* Provident fund

Source: U.S. Social Security Administration, *Social security programs throughout the world — 1995,* Washington, D.C., 1995

UNIT 2: Qualifying period and calculation of benefits

A. Qualifying period

Generally, a qualifying period based on contributions, periods of insurance or employment is required for entitlement to survivors' benefits. The duration of this qualifying period is often the same as that for invalidity or old-age pensions, in view of the fact that survivors' pensions are awarded in the event of the death of a beneficiary who was receiving an invalidity pension or old-age pension, or of an employed person who would have been entitled to a pension at the time of his or her death.

Nevertheless, depending on the country, legislation provides a specific qualifying period which may be either greater or less than the qualifying period stipulated for the old-age pension. One national legislation does not provide for any qualifying period for widows' and orphans' pensions.

B. The benefits

Death grants

In general, social security schemes provide either benefits intended to cover reasonal burial expenses or a lump sum, paid to the members of the family who lived with the deceased or were dependent on him or her, to cover immediate expenses. The payment of such benefit is often subject to the condition that the insured person was, or would have been, entitled to a social security benefit.

In some countries, funeral benefits are only paid in the case of death due to employment injury (accident or occupational disease). For deaths due to other causes, qualifying conditions vary according to national legislation and whether the benefits are linked to the sickness insurance scheme or the pensions scheme. The beneficiaries of death grants include the dependent members of the family of the deceased, or other persons who would have borne the respective costs. The death grant is paid either as a lump sum, or a percentage of the deceased's earnings, usually for one month, sometimes subject to a minimum amount. The award of a death grant to meet all or part of the cost of the funeral of a deceased dependent family member is provided under some schemes, although less commonly.

Uniform-rate pensions

All schemes awarding flat-rate pensions provide survivors' pensions only for widows and orphans. As a rule, in these schemes, the widow's pension amount is equal to that for a single person's old-age pension. It may, however, be higher for certain categories of widows and lower for others. For example, the amount may be higher in the case of widows with dependent children or for the initial period of widowhood. It may be reduced for widows who have not reached the prescribed age for collecting the normal amount of pension or for those who do not have a child.

The amounts for orphans' pensions may vary in relation to the birth order of the children, with the amount for the first child being higher than that for subsequent children. In one country, the amount varies progressively depending on the age of the child.

In countries which have a family allowance scheme, family allowances may be paid in addtion to orphans' pensions, or may replace them (this is the case in at least one country) or may be coordinated with them in other ways.

Earnings-related pensions

Survivors' pensions, paid by schemes in which invalidity and old-age pensions are earnings-related, are usually set at a fraction of the pension to which the deceased person was entitled (or would have been entitled) at the date of his or her death.

The widow's (and where applicable the widower's) pension amounts to a fraction which varies considerably from one scheme to another. It is often set at 50 per cent of the deceased's pension. In some countries, it may be a higher percentage, even as high as 100 per cent. As has already been seen, in some countries the widow's pension is reduced when certain conditions, required for a normal pension, have not been fulfilled; this applies in particular to the age condition. In at least one country, the pension is reduced if the insured person has children who are entitled to an orphans' pension.

The orphan's pension, for a child orphaned of one parent, also amounts to a fraction of the deceased's, which varies from one scheme to another (between 10 and 75 per cent). In the majority of countries, the orphan's pension for a child orphaned of both parents is higher; in many cases, the amount is doubled.

The number of beneficiary children may be limited. As a general rule, the total amount of the survivors' benefits paid in respect of the death of an insured person is subject to a ceiling: the maximum is usually equal to the pension amount to which the deceased person would have been entitled. However, in many countries, the maximum is significantly higher.

The pension for the parents of the deceased may be set in relation to orphans' pension for a child orphaned of one parent, or they may amount to a specific percentage of the deceased person's pension.

Provident funds

Provident funds pay out the balance to the credit of the deceased person (contributions paid plus accrued interest) and they follow the order of priority laid down by the law, where such priority has been established. In principle, the widow is the first beneficiary, unless she had been separated from her husband at the time of his death. The provident funds may, however, be required to make the payment to another person, designated in advance by the person paying the contributions.

PENSION SCHEMES

MODULE 5:
PROVIDENT FUNDS

International Labour Office - Geneva

MODULE CONTENTS

MODULE 5

PROVIDENT FUND OR PENSION SCHEME?

UNIT 1: Origins and characteristics of provident funds

A. Origins of national provident funds

The national provident fund is a form of social security scheme which is found in a number of developing countries. With its' roots in employer-managed savings schemes, the provident fund concept was adopted by most British colonial administrations. Newly-independent countries in Africa, Asia, the Caribbean and the Pacific built on this tradition when establishing the foundations of their social security systems. Coverage of the provident funds was initially restricted to urban workers. As a result of the shift, from an agricultural and largely subsistence economy to a commercial economy based in the urban areas, these workers were no longer able to rely - to the same extent - on the support of the extended family. In many countries, however, the urban workers still maintained close ties with their rural homes and invariably had the intention to return to their villages in old age or when they were no longer able to work.

In their simplest form, national provident funds are compulsory savings schemes. Contributions (usually as a percentage of wages and salaries) from covered employees (i.e. the fund members) and their employers are accumulated in the individual accounts of the members, to which interest is also credited. Benefits are paid out for the long-term social security contingencies (old-age, invalidity and survivorship) usually in the form of a lump sum, although some schemes provide for periodical payments. Many funds also allow withdrawals for other purposes, such as house purchase or permanent emigration. The level of the benefit and the extent of social protection it affords depend upon a number of elements: the length of the period of covered employment; the wages earned; the rate of contribution that was levied on the wages year by year; the amount of interest added to the account annually (according to the fund's investment results and administrative costs); the extent to which the member's balance has been reduced by early withdrawals.

In many ways, the mandatory individual account retirement benefit system, found in Chile and in several other Latin American countries, is similar to a provident fund. The retirement benefits it provides are based entirely on the worker's contributions plus the investment earnings on the fund's assets, less administrative expenses. In this type of retirement system, no social insurance is provided by the scheme because there is no pooling of social risks across workers.

B. Advantages of the national provident funds

At the time of their establishment in the 1950s and 1960s, provident funds were seen as having the following advantages:

- the savings principle was easy to understand;

- the administration was thought to be simple;

- no input of Government funds was necessary;

- the accumulated savings could be invested in national economic development;

- the fund was a supplement to and consistent with support provided through the extended family.

Fig. 12:
Provident funds ...
advantages

In many countries, the provident fund approach was seen as a useful first step towards achievement, at a later stage, of a more effective system of social security. At the time that provident funds were established, the concept of social insurance was already firmly rooted in virtually all industrialized - and a number of developing - countries, for example in Latin America. Newly independent countries of Francophone Africa also adopted the social insurance approach.

The ILO Social Security (Minimum Standards) Convention (No. 102), 1952, established an internationally accepted set of standards for social security schemes. However, national provident funds did not meet those standards in a number of respects. Social insurance pension schemes were generally seen as "something to work towards for the future" by the newly-independent developing countries. Although it was recognized that social insurance schemes provided more comprehensive and adequate protection, they were thought to be inappropriate for the following reasons:

(1)   the central concepts of social insurance, pooling of risks and resources, were thought to be difficult to sell to the workers;

(2)   social insurance schemes were considered to be more complicated to administer and beyond the capacity and resources of the newly-independent countries;

(3)   the payment of pensions to persons, returning to their villages, was considered to be both impractical and less relevant than a lump sum, which the worker could use to establish an income-generating activity and thus provide a future means of support.

Nevertheless, in most countries, it was assumed that the national provident funds would be converted into social insurance schemes after a few years of operation and experience. This has been the case in the Caribbean, where the schemes were small and did not allow for pre-retirement withdrawals.

Table 4 lists the national provident funds by date of legislation and actual implementation.

Table 4: Experience of national provident funds

Region/country	Date established	Date converted	Contribution rate employer/employee (%)
Africa			
Gambia	1981 (1982)		10/5
Ghana	1965	1991	
Kenya	1965		5/5
Nigeria	1961	1994	
Seychelles	1971	1979	
Swaziland	1974		5/5
Tanzania	1964		10/10
Uganda	1967		10/15
Zambia	1965		5/5
Asia			
India	1952	1995	
Indonesia	1951		4/2
Iraq	1956	1964	
Malaysia	1951		12/10
Nepal	1962		
Singapore	1953		20/20
Sri Lanka	1958		12/8
Caribbean			
Dominica	1970	1975 (1976)	
Montserrat	1972		5/5
Saint Christopher and Nevis	1968	1977 (1978)	
Saint Lucia	1970	1978 (1979)	
Saint Vincent	1970	1986	
Pacific			
Fiji	1966		7/7
Kiribati	1976 (1977)		5/5
Papua New Guinea	1980 (1981)		7/5
Solomon Islands	1973 (1976)		7.5/5
Tuvalu	1986		5/5
Vanuatu	1986 (1987)		3/3
Western Samoa	1972		5/5

Sources: U.S. Social Security Administration, *Social security programs throughout the world — 1995,* Washington, D.C., 1995
John Dixon, *National provident funds: The enfant terrible of social security, 1989.*

C. Disadvantages of national provident funds

The experience in operating provident funds has varied considerably in the geographical regions. A few of the countries in Asia and the Pacific provide examples of good administration and investment policy. In other regions, such as Africa, experience of the provident funds has shown, firstly, that their supposed advantages were exaggerated and, secondly, that their disadvantags have been magnified by changing economic and social circumstances.

Fig. 13:
Provident funds ...
disadvantages

Small balances

One of the problems encountered by many provident funds is the low average level of provident fund benefits. The reasons behind this problem are many and complex but among the more obvious causes, which are common to many countries, are:

(1)   the low level of average wages and salaries which are subject to contributions;

(2)   frequent periods of unemployment or uncovered employment, e.g., self-employment; and

(3)   interim withdrawals.

The problem of small balances is particularly acute in the case of premature termination of membership because of death or invalidity. As there is no insurance element, the benefit is not related to the needs or the circumstances of the individual. The provident fund balance may be inadequate when death occurs early in the period of membership. To counter this, some provident funds (e.g. Fiji and Malaysia) have a method of augmenting the death benefit through a formula which takes account of the deceased's age on becoming a member and age at the time of death.

Interim withdrawals

Balances are eroded by what are generally seen by members as one of the advantages of the provident fund system — the interim withdrawal. Such withdrawals are permitted by different schemes, in a wide range of circumstances, but they fall into two categories; loans against the member's balance and permanent withdrawal of all or part of the balance. These withdrawals are often used for current consumption or for the purchase of housing. They have generally been added to the provisions of the scheme, at a later date, in response to the pressure from members who see their balances accumulating at a time when they are experiencing immediate financial difficulty. The personal nature of the provident fund account carries with it the feeling that it is (or should be) accessible to meet other, more immediate, financial obligations.

The desire for early withdrawal, combined with loopholes in the legislation or adminsitrative difficulties, have led to many spurious claims for withdrawal in some countries. Each interim withdrawal, on a provident fund account, reduces the capacity of that account to provide long-term protection in the event of termination of membership. It is this long-term protection which is the primary objective of the scheme. Loans against the balance are seen as an important function of provident funds in some countries and can be compatible with the objectives of the scheme, in relation to old-age protection, provided that the loans are repaid with interest corresponding to the rate of return on investment of the fund.

Administrative difficulties

Although provident funds were regarded at the outset as simple to administer, many such schemes have had great difficulty in maintaining the accounts, crediting interest, collecting contributions from defaulting employers and even in making payments to beneficiaries. The provident fund systems generally provide for balances to be portable, between employments, so that the member receives the total contributed in respect of *all* employment on termination of membership. Such a system requires the member to be identified, by his or her employer and the administration, by means of a membership number. In practice this has proved difficult to achieve. In some schemes many members have been allocated more than one number during their working life. Often it is difficult to trace earlier periods of membership and records contain many seemingly inactive accounts with small deposits. The volume of the administrative task has put a great strain on the resources of many schemes.

Lump-sum payments

The way in which lump-sum payments are spent determines their effectiveness as a means of social security. It was argued that the lump sum would provide the means to acquire an income-generating enterprise which would provide a future source of income. However, in practice, most provident funds do not follow-up with former members or conduct research on how their lump sums are utilized and whether those lump sums do provide a stream of adequate income in retirement. Intuitively it would seem that the beneficiary is much more likely to spend the money on more short-term needs such as children's education or medical expenses. This view is supported by the limited evidence which is available.

Effects of inflation

When provident funds were established the planners could not have anticipated the consequences of inflation and currency devaluation experienced by developing countries in the final quarter of the twentieth century. Inflation hits the effectivness of the lump-sum payment, as a social security instrument, in two ways. While the member is contributing to the scheme, the rate of interest credited to his or her account may not keep pace with the level of inflation. In these circumstances, the lump sum received at the end of membership may represent less, in real terms, than it was worth at the time the contributions were paid. The loss in real terms can be substantial, leading to increased pressure for interim withdrawals, and can bring into question the relevance of the provident fund approach. If inflation continues after the beneficiary has received the lump sum payment, then the real value of whatever benefits are generated, by the disposal of the lump sum, are eroded and there is pressure to use the money for short-term consumption rather than for the future.

If a significant benefit is to be achieved in a reasonable time period, the contribution rate for a provident fund at the outset must be higher than that for a pension scheme. In practice, many provident funds currently have a contribution rate of around 20 percent of covered earnings, with Singapore representing the highest rate at 40 percent (which includes 6 percent for medical benefits). In contrast, depending on the age structure of the insured population and the level of benefits, the contribution rate for a new pension scheme is usually in the range of 7 to 8 percent.

D. *Differences between provident funds and pension schemes*

Certain differences between provident funds and social insurance pension schemes affect possible arrangements for changing from a provident fund to a pension scheme. In the first place, provident funds are *individual* savings schemes, while social insurance pension schemes involve a pooling of risk. Pension schemes are founded on the basis of collective solidarity; in a provident fund, at any time, individual members have a specific balance. In a social insurance pension scheme the participant has an acquired right to a benefit payable in the future, according to a specified formula. A participant's equity in a provident fund at any time is not known. The individual savings approach of a provident fund means there is no subsidy from one member to another or from one generation to another.

Systems of finance

The systems of financing provident funds and social insurance pension schemes are entirely different. Provident funds are fully funded on an individual basis. Social insurance schemes are partially funded, or financed on a pay-as-you-go (PAYG) basis, particularly in industrialized countries. The partial funding of these schemes means that, in the future, contribution rates are expected to rise and that there will be a subsidy from successive generations. Under a partial funding financial system, the contribution rate can be set so that reserve funds are accumulated at a rate commensurate with the expectation of investing them productively.

Investments

Provident funds and social insurance pension schemes both invest in securities guaranteed by the government. Other than this, a provident fund requires no subsidy or guarantee from the Government. Pension schemes do not require a subsidy, although this is found in some schemes, but normally there is a guarantee from the government that promised benefits will be paid. This guarantee provides assurance to participants. But, in practice, it is not often utilized since financing problems in a pension scheme do not occur suddenly. They can be anticipated and corrective measures taken, such as increasing the contribution rate, changing benefit levels or both, before the situation deteriorates to the extent that the Government would be called upon to honour its guarantee.

In a provident fund the investment risk (i.e. the possibility that the provident fund rate of interest paid on members' balances will be lower than the rate of inflation) is borne entirely by the individual members. In a social insurance pension scheme the investment risk (i.e. the possibility that the net rate of investment income on the assets of the scheme will be lower than the rate of inflation) is borne by the scheme; thus it is shared by the participants collectively. The implication of this is that, if a benefit becomes payable during a period when there have been several years with negative real rates of return (years when the rate of inflation has exceeded the rate of interest), new pension scheme benefits will continue to be awarded in accordance with the formula but provident fund lump-sum payments will reflect the loss in the real value of members' balances.

After a provident fund benefit has been paid or pension payments have commenced, the same assumption of the investment risk applies. Whether the beneficiary of a provident fund lump sump applies it so as to retain its real value depends entirely on the beneficiary. Periodic pension payments are generally adjusted to take into account inflation, hence the social insurance pension scheme bears this risk.

Benefits

The benefit in a provident fund is a lump sum equal to the balance in favour of the member. In a pension scheme the total of the periodic payments, in respect of an individual participant, depends on how long the participant - and his or her survivor beneficiaries - live after pension payments commence. Hence the total payments do not bear any direct relationship to the accumulated contributions made in respect of an individual participant.

In a provident fund, from the point of view of the solvency of the fund, it does not matter *when* a member receives the benefit. If an advance or a loan is taken but not repaid, it simply reduces the balance in the member's account. In a social insurance pension scheme, loans to participants, if available, are an investment from the collective fund and they must be repaid or the solvency of the fund can be threatened. Similarly, retirement age has no effect on the solvency of a provident fund. It is, however, a crucial issue in a pension scheme. Provident funds often have retirement ages of 55 or lower. In many countries this is too low a retirement age, for a viable and supportable pension scheme, taking into account the life expectancy of the population which would be covered by the scheme.

UNIT 2: From provident fund to pension scheme

A. *Adaptation of provident funds*

Some provident funds have responded to their apparent disadvantages by introducing changes in the benefits provided. In particular, some schemes offer their members the alternative of periodical payments. These take the form of an annuity based on the final balances or the payment of the final balances by instalments. The Employee's Provident Fund of India, the world's largest, recognized the inadequacies of the benefit provided in the event of premature death. It introduced a special supplementary scheme, which diverted a proportion of the contribution into a separate fund, operated on a risk-pooling basis, from which were paid monthly pensions to survivors at a rate based on the earnings and length of membership of the deceased. This scheme has now been incorporated into the new pension scheme which is the result of converting the employer's contribution into an insurance-based scheme. A social insurance element has been introduced into the Fiji Provident Fund scheme by means of an augmented annuity, which diverts a portion of the contribution income into a special fund. This fund is used for the payment, on request, of a lifetime annuity based on a percentage of the balance in the member's account at retirement age. Nonetheless, in practice few members have opted for this annuity, despite a relatively favourable rate.

In spite of various attempts to broaden their range of protection and become more effective social security institutions, provident funds still suffer from the fundamental dilemma associated with trying to provide adequate social security benefits on the basis of compulsory individual savings. Although they remain popular with their members, because of the reliance on lump-sum payments and the opportunity for interim withdrawals, their inadequacies have become increasingly recognized, in particular because of the effects of inflation. A few more funds have converted to pension schemes in recent years and, in several other countries, conversion is in process or under consideration.

B. Conversion from provident fund to pension scheme

The issue of whether to change from a provident fund to a pension scheme involves questions of a political, socio-economic and even psychological nature. The decision to make the change should be made with the benefit of financial and actuarial advice but, ultimately, it is a policy decision, not a technical matter. A fundamental prerequisite, for the conversion of a provident fund into a social insurance pension scheme, is the recognition of the advantage of such a scheme by the government. Additionally, adequate resources must be made available to enable the conversion to succeed and the scheme to operate successfully.

Fig. 14:

"... obstacles to conversion ... provident fund to pension scheme ..."

Obstacles to conversion

There are also obstacles to conversion, some real and some imagined based on misconceptions.

- Members generally prefer the provident fund lump sum and the opportunity for interim withdrawal, placing priority on their more immediate needs. The strength of this feeling depends on such factors as the age of the member, perceived life expectancy, prospects of employment after withdrawal and the extent of other financial support, for example from the extended family. A further consideration is the extent to which inflation has eroded the real value of the member's balance (and the awareness of this fact).

- The idea of personal ownership of the member's account is still more attractive and more easily understood than the social insurance concept where there is no guarantee of a return of contributions paid on the member's behalf.

- Governments may be hesitant to turn away from a system which generates substantial savings which can be borrowed, at non-competitive rates, for development purposes. However, it is not commonly realized that a pension scheme is capable of generating all the necessary reserves that Government may require. The contribution rate can be set, under the scaled premium system, so as to strike the right balance between the different objectives: a stable contribution rate for a reasonable period in the future; satisfactory benefits, including transition provisions for late-age entrants to the scheme; sufficient reserves, consistent with the opportuntities for investment.

- Many provident funds have experienced serious difficulty in administering their schemes. The changeover to a social insurance scheme is not a panacea for such problems. In fact, the records of the provident fund must be up to date and in order for the conversion to occur. Some provident funds might be reluctant to expose the deficiences in their administration that a conversion would require.

- A social insurance pension scheme requires the availability of sufficient data to enable the completion of an actuarial study prior to the introduction of the scheme. These requirements are considerably in excess of those of a provident fund, where the scheme is obliged to pay out no more than the sum of all the individual accounts.

- The designers of a social insurance scheme may want to provide a higher level of benefits which, in turn, would require a higher contribution rate or an increase in the contribution ceiling. Also, the retirement age under a pension scheme is likely to be significantly higher than under a provident fund scheme.

- The provident fund may be operating with a higher contribution rate than required for a pension scheme, or operating with no contribution ceiling. In this case it would be undesirable to introduce a partially funded or pay-as-you-go pension scheme with a similar contribution structure. It may be difficult to explain why part of the contribution is "unrequired."

Fig. 15:
"Members generally prefer a lump sum"

C. Implementation of conversion

The conversion of a provident fund to a social insurance pension scheme must be preceded by careful planning and extensive consultation and education. It is crucial that the members understand the disadvantages of the provident fund and appreciate the better protection provided by a pension scheme. Sometimes the disadvantages will be apparent, as is the case in those countries where the value of the members' balances have been seriously eroded by inflation. In other countries, where inflation has been modest and where the rate of interest payable to members is comparable to the market rate, workers may cling to the attraction of lump-sum payments. The extent of the education process is directly proportionate to the perceived disadvantages of the provident fund. It will never be possible to convince every member but, at the end of the consultation and education process, Government must take a decision based on what is perceived to be in the best interest of the members.

Transition measures

Replacing a provident fund with a social insurance pension scheme inevitably focuses the members', and consequently the administrators', attention on what is going to happen to their balances in the fund: whether they will be "better off" (get their balances back in periodic payments). Much attention is paid to the transition measures and, unless a long-range perspective is applied, the design of the new pension scheme can be dictated by the need to convince the current provident fund members that they should support the social insurance pension scheme. This approach, while understandable, fails to take into account that, whilst the current provident fund members will be contributors and beneficiaries of the pension scheme for around two generations, the pension scheme will last indefinitely. A generous pension scheme, which may appeal to provident fund members, may create a future burden. It is very difficult to substantially alter benefits in a social security scheme once they have been established. Consequently, once a decision is taken to change from a provident fund to a social insurance pension scheme, the pension scheme should be designed to meet the needs of current *and* future participants, taking into account socio-economic conditions and the capacity of the national economy to support the scheme. The conversion provisions are transitional measures and they are a subsidiary consideration.

Implementation options

The way in which the conversion is implemented will vary from country to country. There are a number of possible ways in which the existing members' accounts can be handled in the conversion process; four are discussed below.

1 - Paying out the provident fund balances

All members to be paid their provident fund balances at the time the pension scheme commences operations. This would be inflationary and would require liquidation of investments which cannot be realized in practice. It is therefore not a viable proposition.

2 - Freezing provident fund balances

Contributions to the provident fund cease and are directed to the pension scheme. Provident fund balances, at the time of the changeover, continue to receive interest and are paid out whenever they become payable under the provident fund regulations. This option would avoid the impossible sudden liquidation of investments required under option 1.

Option 2 has the major deficiency that it would result in the pension scheme starting from the very beginning with participants having no credit for prior service (as does option 1). Under typical pension formulae and qualification requirements it would take a considerable number of years before pensions would become payable - and longer yet before the pensions were a significant proportion of final average earnings. Normally, when a new pension scheme is set up, special transitional provisions are made so as to reduce the qualifying period until the scheme is providing pensions and providing them at adequate levels. These transitional arrangements, which imply a subsidy from later contributors, would be inappropriate since the participants who would be subsidized already have frozen provident fund balances.

3 - Purchase of annuities with provident fund balances

Instead of paying a lump sum from the provident fund, the lump sum is converted into periodic annuity payments. This is an existing option in some provident funds. The amount of the periodic payments depends on the amount of the lump sum, hence it may bear little relationship to a member's final average earnings. Anticipation of the lump-sum payment, through advances or loans which have not been repaid, is reflected in a reduced amount of the periodic payments. It would be possible to calculate the periodical payments so they could be increased to take into account anticipated future increases in the cost of living. However, this would significantly reduce the initial periodical payments. The periodical payments would normally be calculated using actuarial annuity factors and a separate fund would be set up, into which the lump sums would be paid and from which annuity payments would be made. This is an insurance system and the insurance and mortality risks associated with the annuities would be assumed by the fund.

A modification of this approach is the calculation of annuities using factors which are more favourable than actuarial annuity factors. This can encourage members to opt for periodical payments and, presumably, the larger their balances and the more favourable the annuity factors, the more members will exercise this option. The real cost of the periodical payments which are awarded is the actuarial cost. The difference between this and the lump sums which are applied at a favourable rate to calculate the annuity must ultimately be met by the provident fund from a separate fund set up to meet the difference or from other sources.

4 - Conversion of provident fund balances to pension credits

The problems and deficiencies associated with the previous three options for changing from a provident fund to a pension scheme, lead to the conclusion that it is desireable to devise a system, to introduce a social insurance pension scheme, that takes into account:

- prior contributions in the provident fund, so that the pension scheme can be in full operation from its inception and so that adequate pensions are payable;

- the concern of provident fund members over their individual accounts, particularly those members who are near retirement and who have made plans for the utilization of the lump sums;

- that the records which are likely to be available in the provident fund can be used to approximate periods of prior service for the pension scheme; and

- the need to adopt a simple system for conversion, so that members of the provident fund can understand it (especially if there are options) and in order that the social security institution is able to cope with the administration of the conversion system.

The following method of converting a member's provident fund balance into periods of service in the pension scheme is based on the assumption that the annual rate of increase in wages is aproximately equal to the rate of interest credited to provident fund balances. The approximate conversion calculation is the following:

$$\text{Years of service} = \frac{\text{Provident fund balance}}{\text{Final average earnings} \times \text{Provident fund contribution rate}}$$

It is not suggested that this calculation can be applied directly to any provident fund being changed into a social insurance pension scheme. It must be modified to take into account conditions applicable to the particular scheme. Whether the calculation gives reasonable estimates of members' years of contributory service depends on the validity of the assumption that rates of wage increase are approximately equal to rates of interest on the provident fund balances. This must be tested over a period of years in a particular country. The formula provides a simple means of determining the years of service to be credited to the pension scheme, taking into account the data which a provident fund should already have available. It need not be applied until a benefit, under the pension scheme, becomes payable at which time final average earnings data should also be available.

Members of a provident fund, which is converted into a pension scheme in this manner, can be given the option to convert all or part of their provident fund balances into a pension at the time they (or their survivors) qualify for pensions. In order to qualify for a pension, it may be necessary for a portion of the provident fund balances to be converted into years of service in the pension scheme. A member with a significant balance would be able to decide the portion of his or her balance that is to be converted and the remainder would be paid in a lump sum. This conversion procedure would require the pension scheme administration to advise potential pensioners about their options. The procedure is in fact a "mixed system", providing both a pension and possibly a lump sum at the discretion of the beneficiary.

The social insurance institution would have to maintain separate accounts (for the pension fund and the provident fund balances that are frozen) until a member decides how his or her balance is to be applied. Once a provident fund balance is converted, the amount converted would become part of the pension fund reserve. Eventually, over a period of time, the provident fund accounts will all have been converted or paid out.

Another mixed approach is to split the existing contribution rate between a new social insurance pension scheme and a reduced rate provident fund. Part of the "unrequired" contribution could also be used to finance another benefit such as employment injury compensation.

Successful conversions

These techniques have been applied by countries which have already changed from provident funds to pension schemes. In Iraq, the periods of provident fund contributions were fully taken into account by the pension scheme. In Dominica and Grenada, the accumulated individual balances were converted into periods of contributions to the pension scheme, according to a formula. In St. Kitts and St. Vincent, the provident fund balances were frozen. In St. Lucia, provident fund members had all their contributions transferred to the pension fund and received credit towards pension benefits for their actual periods of contribution to the provident fund. In the Seychelles, the provident fund balances were frozen. They continue to receive interest on those balances which are paid to members when they become entitled to a lump sum under the rules of the provident fund.

FURTHER READING

International Labour Office.
Introduction to social security, 3rd edition (Geneva, 1984).

Social insurance and social protection:
Report of the Director General.
International Labour Conference, 80th Session (Geneva, 1993).

"Social security and social protection during periods of stuctural change." Report of the Director-General, Part II.
Eighth African Regional Conference, Mauritius (Geneva, 1993).

International Social Security Association.
Conjugating public and private:
The case of pensions. Studies and research No. 24
(Geneva, 1987).

Survivors' benefits in a changing world.
Studies and research No. 31 (Geneva, 1992).

Iyer, Subramaniam N.
"Pension reform in developing countries."
International Labour Review, Vol. 132, No. 2, 1993, pp. 27-47

Mouton, Pierre.
Social security in Africa: Trends, problems and prospects
(Geneva, 1975).

World Bank.
Averting the old age crisis:
Policies to protect the old and promote growth.
(Washington, DC, Oxford University Press, 1994).

U.S. Social Security Administration.
Social security programs throughout the world – 1995
(Washington, DC, GPO, 1995).

Pension Reform.
A risk strategy:
Reflections on the World Bank Report
"Averting the old age crisis".
Roger Beattie and Warren McGillirray.